12-05

Ancient Greece

Ancient Greece

Other Titles in the World History Series

WORLD HISTORY

Ancient Greece

Don Nardo

LUCENT BOOKS
An imprint of Thomson Gale, a part of The Thomson Corporation

THOMSON
™
GALE

Detroit • New York • San Francisco • San Diego • New Haven, Conn. • Waterville, Maine • London • Munich

LIBRARY OF CONGRESS CATALOGING-IN-PUBLICATION DATA

Nardo, Don, 1947–
    Ancient Greece / by Don Nardo.
       p. cm. — (World history series)
    Audience: Grades 7–8.
    Includes bibliographical references.
    ISBN 1-59018-651-6 (hardcover : alk. paper)
    1. Greece—History—To 146 B.C.—Juvenile literature. I. Title. II. Series.
DF215.N35 2005
938—dc22
                                                                    2005011355

Printed in the United States of America

Contents

Foreword

Each year, on the first day of school, nearly every history teacher faces the task of explaining why his or her students should study history. Many reasons have been given. One is that lessons exist in the past from which contemporary society can benefit and learn. Another is that exploration of the past allows us to see the origins of our customs, ideas, and institutions. Concepts such as democracy, ethnic conflict, or even things as trivial as fashion or mores, have historical roots.

Reasons such as these impress few students, however. If anything, these explanations seem remote and dull to young minds. Yet history is anything but dull. And therein lies what is perhaps the most compelling reason for studying history: History is filled with great stories. The classic themes of literature and drama—love and sacrifice, hatred and revenge, injustice and betrayal, adversity and overcoming adversity—fill the pages of history books, feeding the imagination as well as any of the great works of fiction do.

The story of the Children's Crusade, for example, is one of the most tragic in history. In 1212 Crusader fever hit Europe. A call went out from the pope that all good Christians should journey to Jerusalem to drive out the hated Muslims and return the city to Christian control. Heeding the call, thousands of children made the jour-

ney. Parents bravely allowed many children to go, and entire communities were inspired by the faith of these small Crusaders. Unfortunately, many boarded ships captained by slave traders, who enthusiastically sold the children into slavery as soon as they arrived at their destination. Thousands died from disease, exposure, and starvation on the long march across Europe to the Mediterranean Sea. Others perished at sea.

Another story, from a modern and more familiar place, offers a soul-wrenching view of personal humiliation but also the ability to rise above it. Hatsuye Egami was one of 110,000 Japanese Americans sent to internment camps during World War II. "Since yesterday we Japanese have ceased to be human beings," he wrote in his diary. "We are numbers. We are no longer Egamis, but the number 23324. A tag with that number is on every trunk, suitcase and bag. Tags, also, on our breasts." Despite such dehumanizing treatment, most internees worked hard to control their bitterness. They created workable communities inside the camps and demonstrated again and again their loyalty as Americans.

These are but two of the many stories from history that can be found in the pages of the Lucent Books World History series. All World History titles rely on sound research and verifiable evidence, and all give students a clear sense of time, place, and chronology through maps and time-lines as well as text.

All titles include a wide range of author-itative perspectives that demonstrate the complexity of historical interpretation and sharpen the reader's critical thinking skills. Formally documented quotations and annotated bibliographies enable students to locate and evaluate sources, often instantaneously via the Internet, and serve as valuable tools for further research and debate.

Finally, Lucent's World History titles present rousing good stories, featuring vivid primary source quotations drawn from unique, sometimes obscure sources such as diaries, public records, and con-temporary chronicles. In this way, the voic-es of participants and witnesses as well as important biographers and historians bring the study of history to life. As we are caught up in the lives of others, we are reminded that we too are characters in the ongoing human saga, and we are better prepared for our own roles.

ca. 911–891
The Assyrian Empire begins a period of expansion that will give it control over much of the Near East.

ca. 3000–ca. 1100
Greece's Bronze Age, in which people use tools and weapons made of bronze.

ca. 1200–ca. 1100
The Mycenaean kingdoms and fortresses suffer widespread destruction and rapidly decline.

ca. 800–ca. 500
The Archaic Age, in which city-states rise across Greece.

3000	2500	2000	1500	1000	500

B.C.

ca. 1500–ca. 1400
Mycenaean warlords overthrow another early Aegean people, the Minoans, who have long controlled Crete.

ca. 660
Legendary date for the founding of Japan.

ca. 1550–1069
Years of the New Kingdom in Egypt, in which a series of vigorous kings create an Egyptian empire.

ca. 1100–ca. 800
Greece's Dark Age, in which poverty and illiteracy are widespread.

ca. 563
Siddhartha Gautama, who will later be known as the Buddha, is born in northern India.

The Time of Ancient Greece

334–323
After Philip's assassination, Alexander invades Persia and carves out the largest empire the world has yet seen.

31
The Roman leader Octavian (the future emperor Augustus) defeats the last Greek Hellenistic ruler, Cleopatra, at Actium.

ca. 500–323
Greece's Classical Age, in which Greek arts, architecture, literature, and democratic reforms reach their height.

ca. 221
Chinese emperor Shih Huang Ti orders the construction of the Great Wall of China.

500	400	300	200	100	0

431
Sparta declares war on Athens, initiating the disastrous Peloponnesian War.

323–30
Greece's Hellenistic Age, Greeks continue to fight among themselves and Rome steadily gains control of the Greek world.

480
Darius's son, Xerxes, launches a massive invasion of Greece; in a series of victories, the Greeks expel the Persians.

359
King Philip II takes charge of the culturally backward kingdom of Macedonia and begins forging a formidable army.

490
The Persian ruler Darius sends an expedition to sack Athens, but the Athenians decisively defeat the invaders at Marathon.

The Intrinsic Worth of the Individual

When examining the colorful, exciting panorama of ancient Greek civilization, it is easy to become swept up in the drama of events. The tales of the heroes of the Trojan War battling with bronze swords and spears before the towering stone walls of Troy still capture people's imaginations. The brilliant rise and tragic fall of ancient Athens, a great city with magnificent temples, sculptures, and theaters, remains a fascinating and moving story. And the brave stand made by King Leonidas and his three hundred Spartans against an army of more than 200,000 Persians continues to thrill and excite people.

But such events and achievements are only part of the story of ancient Greece. The Greeks left behind more than a gripping saga of events and the decaying remnants of great art and architecture. Greek ideas—for example, the belief that the truths of nature are not beyond the grasp of the human mind, but are learnable—have survived through the centuries. Other ideas the Greeks introduced became some of the fundamental concepts of modern science, government, and philosophy. Many people today take these concepts for granted without realizing that they originated with the Greeks.

To Shape Their Own Destiny

One of the simplest yet most significant ideas developed and passed on by the Greeks was related to the intrinsic worth of the individual. In ancient lands like Egypt and Mesopotamia, a few kings held absolute power over all of the people. From birth to death, the common person lived in large part to serve the needs and desires of the ruler. Since the concept of individual rights did not exist to any significant degree in these lands, common people had no say in their government. They also had few outlets for individual expression.

In Greece, by contrast, the individual came to be seen as both important and special. In the words of the late historian C.M. Bowra:

> At the center of the Greek outlook lay an unshakable belief in the worth of the individual man. In centuries when large parts of the earth were dominated by . . . absolute monarchies . . . the Greeks were evolving their belief that a man must be respected not as the instrument of an omnipotent overlord, but for his own sake.[1]

The recognition of the worth of the individual opened up whole new avenues of thought and action. People came to believe that their own needs and desires were important and that they had a right to

Pericles of Athens was a champion of democracy, a system based in large degree on the Greek concept of the intrinsic worth of the individual.

shape their own destiny. From this view evolved the concept of democracy, the rule by and for the people. Individual creative expression also blossomed, leading to great achievements in art, literature, and philosophy. In addition, the Greeks paved the way for the development of science with their belief that the power of an individual's mind could reveal the truths of nature. Admittedly, some Greeks—women, for example—were not allowed the right to take part in government or allowed much in the way of individual expression. Still, the fact that a sizable segment of the population did enjoy these rights was bold and revolutionary at the time.

The Fabric of Western Tradition

Indeed, the complex saga of Greek history, which still inspires and enriches the modern world, was driven to a significant degree by this simple and noble concept of human individuality. And thanks to the cultural influence the Greeks exerted on the rest of the ancient world, that concept took root in other cultures. From Greece, noted scholar C.E. Robinson suggests,

It was carried outwards by Alexander's conquests to the East, then to Rome and the West, till it came at last to permeate most of the civilized world. . . . Without that heritage [of the intrinsic worth of the individual], modern civilization would be something quite other than what it is. The whole fabric of [Western, or European-based] tradition is rooted in the doctrine . . . that the state exists for the individual, not the individual for the state . . . [and that] the individual [has the right] to think his own thoughts, to utter them in public, and . . . to act in accordance with his own private conscience. This conception we owe to the Greeks.[2]

Chapter One

The Birth of Greek Civilization

Jutting down from southern Europe into the eastern Mediterranean Sea is the arid, mountainous land of Greece. Though small—only about the size of New York State—Greece has greatly contributed to the development of human culture. In the sixth, fifth, and fourth centuries B.C., the Greeks created a brilliant and remarkable civilization. Referred to today as the Classical Age, this was the era when Greek art, architecture, and philosophy reached their peak. It was the Greece of Pericles, the distinguished statesman and builder; of great playwrights such as Aeschylus and Sophocles; and of original thinkers like Socrates and Plato. The influence of this magnificent culture on later cultures was profound and long lasting. Greek art and ideas helped to shape Western civilization. And they remain a powerful inspiration to people around the world today.

The appearance of the splendid culture of classical Greece was not a sudden or chance occurrence. Instead, it grew out of many centuries of Greek civilization stretching back into the Bronze Age, the era—lasting from about 3000 to 1100 B.C.—in which people used weapons and tools made of bronze. The classical Greeks called this dimly-remembered period in their past the Age of Heroes.

Minoan Builders and Traders

The first advanced culture in Greece, and indeed in all of Europe, was created by a people referred to today as the Minoans. Their civilization flourished from about 2200 to 1450 B.C. on Crete, the large island located about one hundred miles southeast of the Greek mainland. The Minoans built huge, splendid palaces. For example, some sections of the palace at Knossos, their chief city, located near the northern coast of the island, were five stories high. The entire complex featured hundreds of interconnected rooms. As many as thirty

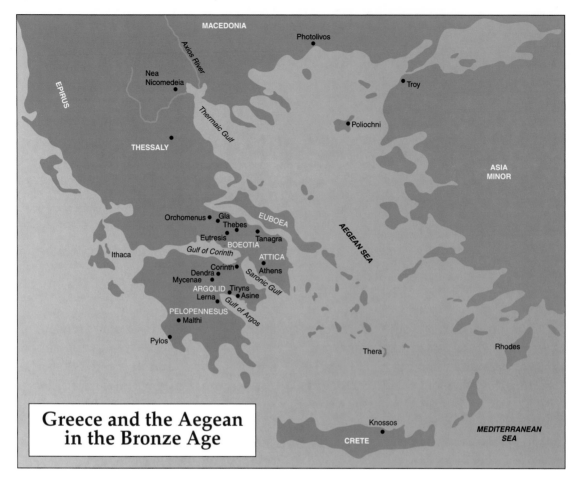

Greece and the Aegean in the Bronze Age

to fifty thousand people lived in the town and villages that surrounded it. And there were dozens, perhaps hundreds, of Minoan towns on Crete and the islands of the Aegean Sea (the inlet of the Mediterranean Sea bordering eastern Greece).

There is evidence that the larger Minoan structures were highly sophisticated buildings with modern-style plumbing features, such as clay pipes that carried water from room to room. The Minoans even had toilets. "Wastes were flushed away," scholar Maitland Edey says, "by pouring water down an elaborate system of drains that included clay pipes carefully fitted together in sections and stone troughs to carry off rain water."[3]

Minoan sophistication in building and art was matched by the size and complexity of the trading fleets and networks the Minoans maintained. The cities of Crete traded with one another. The Minoans also established colonies in the Aegean islands and traded with foreigners living far beyond. Minoan ships made frequent trips to mainland Greece and southern Italy in the west, Troy in northwestern Asia Minor (what is now Turkey), the coasts of southern Asia Minor, the large island of Cyprus (lying south of Asia Minor), and the coasts of Palestine and Egypt far to the south of Cyprus. Evidence for Minoan contacts with Egypt takes the form of paintings of Minoan traders found in several Egyptian tombs. The Egyptians called the Minoans the "Keftiu."

Unearthing the Truth Behind the Legend

Because the Minoans kept few records and no histories, their culture had been largely forgotten by the time of the classical Greeks. Yet a few vague memories of the Minoan era remained, passed on by word of mouth over the course of many centuries. Exaggerated and romanticized by repeated tellings, some Minoan cities, people, and events survived as legends and myths. After the decline of classical Greece, most people assumed that these myths were purely fanciful. Only in modern times did archaeologists discover that many of these stories had a basis in fact.

Perhaps the most famous myth about Minoan times concerned King Minos, who ruled a great kingdom from his splendid palace in the city of Knossos. Supposedly, even cities on the Greek mainland, such as Athens, came under his domination.

A modern reconstruction of the Minoan palace-center at Knossos shows that it was a complex, highly sophisticated structure.

Under, or within, Minos's palace, in a huge maze called the Labyrinth, dwelled the Minotaur, a monster that was half-human and half-bull. The king regularly appeased the fearsome creature by feeding it young Athenian men and women. But eventually, an Athenian hero named Theseus traveled to Crete, determined to defeat Minos and kill the Minotaur. As the first-century-A.D. Greek biographer Plutarch described it:

Theseus was able to seize the harbor [near Knossos], disembark his men,

and reach Knossos before his arrival was discovered. There he fought a battle at the gates of the Labyrinth. As Ariadne [Minos's daughter] now succeeded to the throne, he made a truce with her, recovered the young Athenians, and concluded a pact of friendship between the Athenians and the Cretans, who swore that they would never in the future begin a war with Athens.[4]

For dozens of centuries, the tale of Minos's Labyrinth, the bull-monster that

A surviving fresco—a painting done on wet plaster—shows Minoan youths vaulting over a bull. The exact meaning of this ritual remains unknown.

A painting by historian-artist Peter Connolly shows Theseus's ship landing on Crete. Theseus went on to kill the fearsome minotaur.

dwelled in it, and the war with Athens remained mere myth. Then, in the year 1900 British archaeologist Sir Arthur Evans began excavating at the legendary site of Knossos. He reasoned that the large and complex palacelike structure he found there could easily have served as a model for the mythical Labyrinth. The palace was adorned with numerous paintings and sculptures depicting bull worship. Evans and other scholars suggested that priests wearing bull's horns or masks may have inspired the myth of the half-human Minotaur. Because the evidence found at Knossos conformed to the legend of King Minos so closely, Evans dubbed the early Greeks who built the city Minoan.

The Mainland Mycenaeans

Mounting evidence also showed that the mythical war with the mainlanders may have been based on fact as well. During the same centuries that the Minoans thrived on Crete, another group of early Greeks, the Mycenaeans, lived on the Greek mainland. Their name comes from their chief fortress-city of Mycenae, located in a hilly area of southeastern Greece.

A reconstruction shows the citadel at Mycenae in its prime (above). The photo at right shows the citadel's ruins today.

Other Mycenaean towns, including Tiryns, Pylos, and Athens, each ruled by its own king, dotted southern Greece.

The palace-citadels that dominated these towns were considerably smaller and less sophisticated than the Minoan palace centers. However, the mainland fortresses had more formidable defenses. Some of the citadel walls were 10 feet (3m) thick, and several of the stones used in the construction of the tombs of the Mycenaean kings weighed up to 120 tons (109 metric tons)

each. In fact, many of the Mycenaeans' building stones were so large that some of the classical Greeks who later visited the ruins of Mycenae thought it had been erected by a race of giants.

Some evidence suggests that, as in the ancient myths, the Minoans on Crete long influenced and perhaps even militarily dominated the Mycenaeans on the mainland. Certainly numerous mainland customs and styles of dress were similar to those of Crete. One important difference between the two peoples was that the Mycenaeans spoke an early form of Greek, whereas the Minoans spoke a completely different language that scholars have yet to identify. The Mycenaeans also appear to have been more regimented, militaristic, and warlike than the Minoans. But as long as the powerful Minoan navy controlled the Aegean, as it did for several centuries, the Mycenaeans had little hope of expanding their power base beyond the mainland.

An Unprecedented Disaster

Scholars are not yet sure what caused the decline of Minoan naval power and allowed the subsequent conquest of the Minoan sphere by the Mycenaeans in the fifteenth and fourteenth centuries B.C. However, evidence suggests that this major shift in the balance of power in the Bronze Age Aegean was at least partly due to natural causes. The culprit lay on the small island of Thera (today called Santorini), located about seventy miles north of Crete. Sometime between about 1620 and 1450 B.C. the long dormant volcano on the island suddenly sprang to life and erupted with unprecedented violence.

Ash spewed skyward from the mountain and darkened the skies over much of the eastern Mediterranean.

Eventually, the main section of the volcano collapsed violently, causing an enormous displacement of water. This produced giant tsunamis that had far more destructive power than the ones that devastated Indonesia and Thailand in December 2004. "If we concede," Edey writes,

> that most . . . of Crete's ships were swamped in the harbors around the island, crippling her defenses and reducing her ability to trade overseas; if we assume that the agricultural basis of the country's economy was jolted by a disastrous ashfall that blanketed the eastern half of Crete; if, in short, we presume a number of volcanic events on Thera doing one thing or another to start a downward slide in the Minoan economy, then we begin to see how [Minoan power declined].[5]

The Thera eruption, the worst natural disaster in recorded history, was so terrible that the memory of it became part of the legends passed down through the generations to the classical Greeks. More than a thousand years after the catastrophe, the Greek philosopher Plato recorded these legends in his tale of Atlantis, a great seafaring island nation that sank into the sea.

Even if based on fact, this legend was an exaggeration. Though crippled by the catastrophe, the Minoans managed to sur-

The Mycenaean Economic System

The Mycenaeans, like the Minoans, practiced what today is called a collective form of agriculture, in which a central authority monitors, collects, and redistributes the output of the farmers and craftspeople. The system had a pyramid-like form, say scholars Carol G. Thomas and Craig Conant in their book Citadel to City-State.

At its base, the great majority of the population labored in their small fields to produce a surplus, which was gathered for collective storage within the protected citadel. Between the base and apex [of the pyramid] was a smaller though still sizable group of craftsmen and merchants, much of whose labor [was] monopolized by the palace in return for rations produced by the peasants. At the top of the pyramid were the administrative and military elites and the central manager, named in the palace records as the *wanax*. . . . The *wanax* and his peers provided security against famine and protection against enemies for those situated lower on the pyramid.

A nineteenth-century artist created this impression of the island of Thera during the 1866 eruption of its volcano. The ancient eruption was far larger than this.

vive it. Evidence shows that they slowly began to rebuild their stricken towns and lost ships. However, they never fully recovered. In the 1400s B.C., the Mycenaeans took advantage of their neighbors' weakened state by invading Crete and taking control of the surviving Minoan settlements.

The Trojan War

In the roughly three centuries following their takeover of Crete, the Mycenaean warlords controlled the Aegean seaways. They benefited from commerce with some of the same peoples the Minoans had traded with. In addition, the Mycenaeans made part of their living by raiding. Among the targets of these raids were undoubtedly some of the islands and cities along the coasts of Asia Minor.

One of these cities, Troy, may have been attacked and sacked by an alliance of Mycenaean kings. The legendary eighth-century-B.C. Greek poet Homer told about such an event in his epic poem the *Iliad*. In the story told in that and other early Greek poems, the Greeks fought to rescue Helen, wife of King Menelaus of Sparta, after she had been abducted by Paris, a Trojan prince. The siege lasted ten years, and the Greeks finally used a trick to gain entrance

This reconstruction of Troy in the Bronze Age shows why it was so difficult to capture. It had high walls and was built atop a steep hill.

into the city. They constructed a huge wooden horse, left it as a gift to the gods, and then pretended to leave. The Trojans dragged the horse into Troy, unaware that Greek warriors were hiding inside. That night, as the Trojans slept, the Greeks climbed out of the horse and opened the gates for their army.

Many scholars have tried to determine whether the Trojan War was a real event. Evidence uncovered in Troy's ruins indicates that the city did undergo a siege in about 1220 B.C., the approximate period in which the mythical Trojan War supposedly took place. However, it remains unproven that this was the siege described

by Homer or, for that matter, that the war in the *Iliad* ever actually took place.

History Becomes Legend

If this legendary attack on Troy was a real event, it was one of the last successful ventures of the Mycenaeans. Sometime between 1200 and 1150 B.C., the Aegean sphere, as well as many parts of the Near East, underwent a period of tremendous upheaval. Most of the major Mycenaean strongholds were sacked and burned, never to be rebuilt.

Historians have proposed a number of theories to explain this turmoil, including civil conflicts and a disruption of farming and trade leading to the ruin of the palace economies. Scholar Thomas R. Martin here summarizes a more recent explanation (suggested by Vanderbilt University scholar Robert Drews):

Previously, the preponderance of military might [in the Mycenaean kingdoms] had lain with . . . chariots carrying archers. . . . These chariot forces had been supplemented by infantrymen, mostly foreign mercenaries. . . . These hired foot soldiers [eventually] realized that they could use their long swords and javelins to defeat the chariot forces in direct battle by swarming in a mass against their vehicle-mounted overlords. Emboldened . . . and motivated by a lust for booty, the motley bands of mercenaries attacked [the palaces and

Bronze Age Charioteers and Their Armor

The exact nature of warfare in Bronze Age Greece is uncertain. Archaeological evidence shows that soldiers used bronze swords, bronze-tipped spears, and bows and arrows. Other evidence suggests that some chariots were used in war, though it is unclear how many were involved and how the warriors mounted on them fought and defended themselves. Some tantalizing clues come from examinations of surviving paintings, sculptures, and remnants of armor from the period. The paintings and sculptures show charioteers firing powerful bows and wearing armored outfits made of copper or bronze scales sewn or glued to leather or linen jerkins. More impressive is a massive suit of bronze plate armor (not unlike that of a medieval knight) discovered in 1960 at Dendra, near Mycenae. Such armor was much too expensive for use by average soldiers and must have been worn by a few elite fighters. Also, the Dendra armor was far too heavy and inflexible for a foot soldier; it would have been very practical as protection against a rain of arrows for a man standing on a chariot.

Accompanied by his driver, a Mycenaean warrior heads for battle. He wears a suit of bronze plate armor like the one discovered at Dendra.

towns]. . . . With no firm organization among themselves, the rebels fatally weakened the civilizations they betrayed.[6]

Whatever the cause or causes of the disaster, Greek civilization suddenly declined and entered a cultural dark age. No longer inhabited and kept up, the citadels at Mycenae, Tiryns, and other mainland sites began to decay, while literacy, record keeping, artistic skills, and other factors that had supported Bronze Age society were lost. In this way, Greece's magnificent Bronze Age civilization passed into legend. Memories of real people and events

According to legend, after the Trojans dragged the wooden horse into their city, Greek warriors climbed out and opened the gates for their own army.

Proof That the Mycenaeans Spoke Greek

Archaeologists found examples of a writing system, which they named Linear B, in the ruins excavated at many Bronze Age sites. No one could read the script until British scholar Michael Ventris deciphered it in the 1950s, as described by Sarah Pomeroy and her colleagues in their political, social, and cultural history of Greece.

The tablets presented an enormous challenge, because the script was totally unlike any of the other writing systems in use among the Late Bronze Age civilizations, and no one knew what the underlying language was. Relatively little progress was made until the early fifties, when . . . Michael Ventris broke the code. Working from the hypothesis that the signs stood for whole syllables rather than single letters and that the language might possibly be Greek . . . Ventris was gradually able to obtain the phonetic values of some of the signs. For example, a combination of three signs— *ti-ri-po*— yields the syllabic equivalent of the Greek word *tripous* ("tripod"). In 1953, Ventris and a collaborator, John Chadwick of Cambridge University, jointly published their findings in a famous article that has completely changed our picture of the Bronze Age Aegean. It is now certain beyond any doubt that Greek was the language of the Mycenaean culture.

grew increasingly dim and distorted until they became colorful, romantic tales of an era in which heroes, monsters, and gods roamed the land.

Meanwhile, the surviving Greeks steadily forgot their heritage. And small groups of them came to identify themselves only with the isolated valley or island where they lived. They became poor farmers, fishermen, and shepherds. But the glories of Aegean civilization were not over. In time, the descendants of these Greek-speaking folk would build a new civilization, one that would greatly surpass that of the bronze-clad heroes of their myths.

Chapter Two

The Rise of City-States

During the three centuries that followed the collapse of Mycenaean civilization in the 1100s B.C., Greek civilization reached its lowest point. When the Minoan and Mycenaean cultures disappeared, so too did their prosperous trade network, writing, arts, architecture, and many of their crafts. Along with cultural stagnation came widespread poverty. The vast majority of people were able to survive through fishing and growing whatever crops they could in the country's mostly thin, rocky soil. Overall, a sort of dark age descended on the Greek lands.

Eventually, the Greeks recovered, though it was a slow, often difficult process that took centuries. Not until the eighth century B.C. did commerce and living standards begin to reach levels comparable to those before the Dark Age. Also, the society that emerged was very different than that of the Bronze Age. In place of kingdoms ruled by all-powerful warlords rose hun-

dreds of small city-states, the governments of which increasingly came to be controlled by the common people.

Life in Greece's Dark Age

Foreshadowings of the dynamic new civilization that would eventually rise from the wreckage of the old Bronze Age can be seen in Greece's Dark Age. Indeed, the region was neither primitive nor stagnant during the Dark Age, as new ideas and skills periodically filtered in from the outside. One of the most important was iron smelting, which spread across Greece between about 1050 and 950 B.C. (This skill probably came from the Near East, where it had long been known, and entered the Greek sphere via Cyprus, the large island lying south of Asia Minor.) Iron use was a major advance, since tools and weapons made of that metal are tougher and keep their edges better than those made of bronze.

The early years of Greece's Dark Age also witnessed large population movements. The reasons for these migrations are not completely clear, but many mainland Greeks appear to have been displaced by other peoples entering Greece. These included the tribal Dorians from the Balkan region south of the Danube River. Many of those who were displaced crossed the Aegean and settled on the coasts of western Asia Minor, which later came to be called Greek Ionia. Other mainlanders may have migrated in search of better farmland and other opportunities for a fresh start.

In contrast to the palace centers and large towns of Mycenaean times, social and political life during the Dark Age was centered around individual villages. Each village had a local leader called a *basileus.* "The Greek word *basileus* is usually translated as 'king' wherever it appears in literature, including [Homer's] *Iliad* and *Odyssey*," noted scholar Sarah Pomeroy points out.

> It would be misleading, however, to call the Dark Age leaders "kings," a title that conjures up in the modern mind visions of monarchs with autocratic powers. A more appropriate name for the Dark Age *basileus* is the . . . term "chief," which suggests a man with far less power than a king. The *basileus,* nevertheless, was a man of great stature and importance in the community.[7]

The governing institutions for villages described in Homer's epic poems, which scholars believe roughly reflect those that existed in the late Dark Age, were fairly simple. A local chief met with a few advis-ers and assistants (almost surely all leading citizens) in a council (*boule*) to decide policy for the whole community or people (*demos*). To achieve a consensus in the community, the chief and his associates presented their ideas and decisions to an assembly of fighting men, who gave their approval. The chief probably also led public sacrifices to the gods and occasionally met with chiefs from neighboring regions.

As portrayed in Homer's works, society was male dominated. It was also characterized by a competitive spirit, the desire to be recognized as "best" (*aristos*) and thereby to acquire honor and respect. As time went on, the term *aristos* came to be applied to the wealthiest and most successful men, hence their designation as aristocrats and their social class as the aristocracy. Meanwhile, as would prevail in most later ages in Greece, women had no political voice. Treated as second-class citizens, they remained under the strict control of their fathers, husbands, and other male relatives.

Expanded Prosperity in the Archaic Age

The village-oriented society of the Dark Age was bound to change as Greece's population, trade networks, and prosperity all steadily increased over time. This stimulated the development of several larger towns. Each became the focus of a new sociopolitical unit, the city-state, which the Greeks called the polis. Modern scholars refer to the era in which full-blown city-states emerged across the Greek sphere as the Archaic Age (ca. 800–ca. 500 B.C.).

The average Greek city-state consisted of a central town, or urban center, which was often built around a central hill (acropolis), which was fortified in case the community was attacked. The urban center was surrounded by small villages and sometimes extensive farmlands. Each polis viewed itself as a tiny, separate nation and guarded its borders and local traditions fiercely. Among the more influential and powerful poleis that emerged in Archaic times were Athens, on the Attic Peninsula; Thebes, which dominated Boeotia (bee-OH-shya), the region lying north of Attica; Corinth, Argos, and Sparta, all in the Peloponnesus (the large peninsula making up the southern third of mainland Greece); and Samos and Miletus, in Ionia.

Greece's new prosperity and expanded local populations stimulated these and

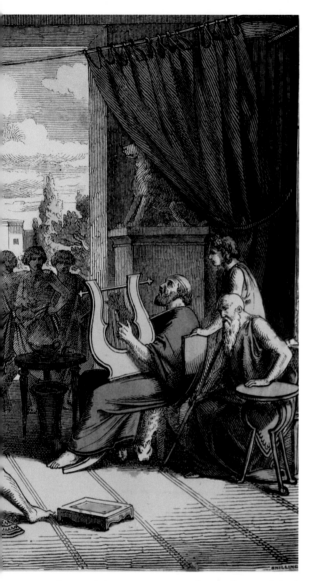

other cities to expand and establish colonies. For about two hundred years, the Greeks founded numerous colonies along the coasts of the Aegean, Mediterranean, and Black seas. Two of the most successful of these overseas poleis were Byzantium, located near the entrance to the Black Sea, and Syracuse, on the western edge of the island of Sicily, directly south of Italy. So many prosperous Greek colonies sprang

up in Sicily and southern Italy that the region later became known (in Latin) as Magna Graecia, or "Greater Greece."

Early Political Experimentation

Increased prosperity also helped bring about profound changes in the political structure of many Greek poleis. In most poleis, power passed from the hands of village chieftains to the councils that had once assisted and advised them. The men on these councils were at first all aristocrats. This form of government is known as an oligarchy (from a Greek word meaning "rule of the few"). Some states, a prominent example being Corinth, retained their oligarchic councils for a long time.

In many other Greek states, however, the common people steadily grew disenchanted with aristocratic rule and new forms of government evolved. Beginning in the mid-600s B.C., for instance, ambitious individuals in several leading cities gained power by exploiting growing anti-aristocratic sentiments. The Greeks came to call these men tyrants. (The familiar negative image of a tyrant—a cruel or oppressive dictator—developed later.) A number of Greek tyrants, at least at first, were law-abiding, generous, and effective rulers who tried to maintain the support of the people by sponsoring the arts and public building projects. Among the more successful tyrants were Peisistratus, who gained control of Athens in 561 B.C., and Polycrates, who took power in Samos about 540 B.C.

As a form of government, however, tyranny was unstable and short-lived in Greece. This is because a tyrant, well meaning or not, was an absolute ruler who needed popular support—particularly the backing of the local soldiers—to stay in power. The citizen bodies of many city-states, which included the soldiers, increasingly came to eliminate the tyrants and to assume governing authority themselves.

Indeed, in most Greek city-states the soldiers did not belong to an elite class separate from ordinary citizens; rather, they actually made up the single most populous sector of the citizen body. Agricultural changes in the late Dark Age and early Archaic Age promoted the

spread of small farmers, who were tough, independent men who neither needed nor wanted control by aristocratic or other ruling elites.

These farmers became not only the economic backbone of each polis but also, in the role of militiamen, the source of its military strength. In an emergency, they took up arms to protect their own lands and the greater community, then returned to their farms when the crisis was over. When clad in heavy armor, they were called hoplites. And they developed a unique and highly effective form of warfare based on a battlefield formation known as the phalanx. Wielding round bronze shields, thrusting spears, and short swords, the hoplites stood in rows, one behind the other, and marched forward in unison. Usually, the only force that could

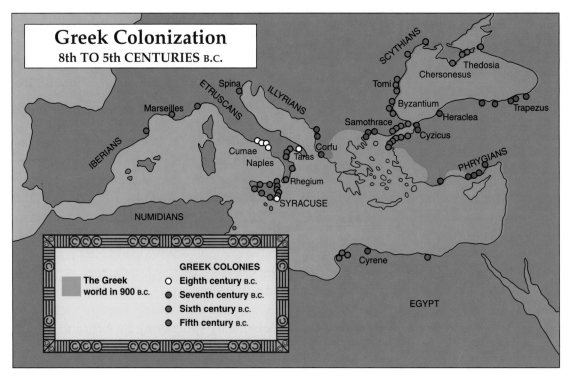

Greek Colonization
8th TO 5th CENTURIES B.C.

GREEK COLONIES
The Greek world in 900 B.C.
○ Eighth century B.C.
◑ Seventh century B.C.
◑ Sixth century B.C.
● Fifth century B.C.

The Hoplite's Shield

The term *hoplite* may derive from the Greek word *hopla*, meaning "heavy equipment." "Heavy" is certainly appropriate in describing a hoplite, for his body armor and shield often weighed forty to fifty pounds or more. For this reason, hoplites were designated as "heavy infantry," a common term in Western warfare ever since.

The hoplite's shield (*hoplon* or *aspis*) was about three feet in diameter and weighed roughly 17 to 18 pounds (7.7 to 8.2 kg). It was gently concave (curved inwards) with a wooden core reinforced on the outside by a coating of bronze, or sometimes by layers of ox hide. The inside of such a shield was lined with leather and featured a distinctive gripping system. The system consisted of a bronze strip with a loop, the *porpax*, in the middle, through which the hoplite passed his left forearm, and a leather handle, the *antilabe*, which he grasped with his left hand. Because the hoplite's shield rested on his arm, he could let go of the *antilabe* and hold a spare weapon in his left hand without losing the shield. This ingenious gripping system also helped to relieve the burden of the shield's considerable weight.

This reconstruction by Peter Connolly shows a Spartan hoplite, circa 500 B.C., carrying his shield on his back.

---

withstand the frontal assault of a phalanx was another phalanx.

During the mid-to-late Archaic era, Sparta developed the most effective and widely feared hoplites and phalanx in Greece. This was partly because the Spartans did not, as so many other Greeks did, devote their main energies to rapid social and political change. Sparta maintained a conservative government headed by two kings who ruled jointly (aided by a council of elders). And Spartan society was highly regimented, with a strong focus on the *agoge*, a harsh but effective

The Greek phalanx, seen here in action against a foreign foe, consisted of rows of soldiers who acted in concert, protecting and encouraging one another as they penetrated enemy lines.

system of military training for young men that began at age seven. Increasingly isolated from Greece's cultural and political mainstream, the Spartans came to distrust change and preferred to have as little contact with outsiders as possible.

In contrast, many other Greek city-states encouraged individualism and change. Athens took the early lead in instituting governmental reforms. In 621 B.C., responding to the demands of the city's citizens, a prominent citizen named Draco drew up a set of laws. But these were widely seen

as too harsh, so in 594 B.C. another leading citizen, Solon, spearheaded reforms that repealed most of Draco's laws and replaced them with more moderate ones. Men of all classes, including those who did not own land, were allowed to vote in Athens's Assembly. Solon also created the Council (*Boule*). Made up of four hundred men chosen by lot (random drawing), this body drew up the list of topics to be discussed by the Assembly. These were important steps toward full-blown democracy, which would develop in Athens later.

Greek Temples and Oracles

During the centuries in which the Greek city-states evolved and people began to worship the Olympian gods, ways of worshipping these gods also developed. Among the religious institutions that all Greeks recognized were temples and oracles. Each Greek temple was a sacred building dedicated to a specific god who, worshippers believed, periodically visited and rested within the building. To respect the god's privacy, therefore, worship took place at altars set up outside the temple rather than inside. The main interior room (cella) of a temple was dominated by the cult image of the deity, usually a large statue.

Over time, special religious temples and shrines appeared in Greece that all of the various city-states considered their common property. The most important and famous of these was at Delphi, located a few miles north of the Gulf of Corinth in central Greece. The temple at Delphi was dedicated to the god Apollo. People from all over Greece journeyed there to consult the oracle, the shrine's priestess. Most people believed she was a medium through which Apollo and other gods spoke directly to humans. Those seeking advice made donations to pay for the temple's and oracle's upkeep. A few other Greek shrines had oracles as well, but none were as revered as the one at Delphi.

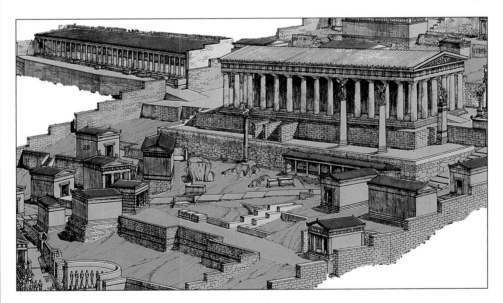

In this modern reconstruction of the religious precinct at Delphi, the Temple of Apollo is at the upper right.

A seventeenth-century painting depicts the Athenian statesman Solon presenting his revised version of Draco's law code to the city's leaders.

Linked by Language

The political and other differences between Athens and Sparta illustrate how much customs and institutions could vary from one polis to another. Yet in spite of these differences, Greeks everywhere recognized that they shared common origins and a common culture. First, they all spoke Greek. Though separate dialects developed in various parts of the land, all Greeks could easily communicate and share ideas. They all called the general region they inhabited Hellas and themselves Hellenes. Their common language, the Greeks felt, separated them from foreigners, whom they referred to as barbarians. (The initial meaning of this term was

the fairly neutral "non–Greek speakers," but over time it came to be used in more negative and insulting ways.)

In addition to spoken Greek, written Greek appeared for the first time in the Archaic Age. Sometime in the 700s B.C., the Greeks, who had been illiterate since the Bronze Age, adopted an alphabet used by a Near Eastern people, the Phoenicians. The Phoenician system had twenty letters, each representing a particular sound. Stringing the letters together in various combinations could produce most of the words in the language. The major drawback was that all of the letters were consonants. The combination *mt*, for example, might stand for "mat," "moat," or "meet," and so the reader had to deduce the meaning from the context of the sentence. The Greeks eliminated this problem by adding vowels to the alphabet.

Other Aspects of Shared Culture

Another thing all Greeks had in common was their heritage of myths about the Age of Heroes. The story told in Homer's *Iliad*, in particular, portrayed the Greeks banding together into a single army with a common goal. Though the Greeks of the Archaic Age lived separately and often fought with one another, they retained this memory of a time when they were united.

Religion was another significant cultural link among the emerging Greek city-states. During the Dark Age, tales of various gods from the heroic period survived in myths and epic poems, and people all over Greece came to accept these gods. They recognized Zeus as the chief god. He ruled over both heaven and Earth, and his symbols were the thunderbolt and the eagle. Other important gods and goddesses included Apollo, god of prophecy, truth, healing, and music; Poseidon, who ruled the seas and caused earthquakes; Aphrodite, goddess of love and beauty; and Artemis, who ruled the night and governed the animals. Most Greeks in these early times believed that the leading gods dwelled on top of Mount Olympus, the highest mountain in Greece (located in the northern sector of the mainland).

The Greeks did not envision their gods as perfect deities. The gods, like people, sometimes made mistakes. Also like humans, the Greek gods fought among themselves; had marriages, love affairs, and children; and expressed emotions such as hate, pity, and greed. The humanness of the gods did not bother the Greeks. In fact, people felt that they could relate better to the gods precisely because these divinities acted so much like humans. Also, the often frivolous behavior of the gods was much less important to the Greeks than the power these deities held. "Though Greek gods might seem to modern minds often to fall below the standards demanded of divinity," C.M. Bowra pointed out,

> they had something impressive in common. They were all to a high degree embodiments of power, whether in the physical world or in the mind of man. From them came literally everything, both visible and invisible, and it was the task of the mortals to make the proper use of what the gods provided. The Greeks . . . did not expect them to follow the rules of human behavior. What counted was their power.[8]

The Greeks also had in common special public religious festivals that were attended by people from city-states far and wide. Often large-scale athletic competitions were held at these festivals, the most famous of which was the Olympic Games, dedicated to Zeus. Beginning in 776 B.C. (according to tradition), these contests were staged every four years at Olympia, in the western part of the Peloponnesus. The Olympics became so important to the Greeks that even during wartime soldiers of enemy states observed an international truce long enough for everyone to compete peacefully.

The Olympics and the Competitive Spirit

The Olympic Games were one of the most important Panhellenic, or all-Greek, activities that developed in Archaic times. The importance and sanctity of the Games to Greeks far and wide was demonstrated by the Olympic truce. In the months leading up to the great event, three special heralds from Elis, the city-state that hosted the contests, visited every Greek state. They not only invited all to attend the Games but also announced the truce, eventually lasting three months, during which all participating states were forbidden to make war. This was done to ensure safe passage for the thousands of competitors, spectators, and religious pilgrims who attended the Games. Violations were rare and resulted in exclusion from the Games and/or heavy fines.

Love of sport was not the only reason these athletes from many states came together. The Olympics were also important as an outlet for the Greeks' intense competitive spirit and desire to achieve honor and prestige. Winning athletes always received numerous financial and other awards when they returned to their home cities. Moreover, a number of poleis rewarded victorious native sons with free meals for life. And the most successful athletes became the subjects of heroic songs and statues.

Danger from the East

Thus, in the six hundred years following the breakdown of Mycenaean society, the Greeks built a rich, vibrant, and prosperous civilization. One reason that the city-states enjoyed such steady growth and development for so long was that no outside power hindered them. Large empires to the south and east of Greece, such as Egypt and Assyria, saw the tiny Greek cities as faraway and unimportant. For a long time, therefore, these great powers left the Greeks alone. But toward the end of the sixth century B.C., a new power rose in the east. The mighty Persian Empire expanded outward like a giant wave, subduing culture after culture. Eventually, that ominous wave threatened to spread across the Aegean, annihilate the Greeks, and engulf the rest of Europe.

Chapter Three

Democracy and Empire: Athens Ascendant

No single word can adequately describe Greece's Classical Age (ca. 500–323 B.C.). But if one had to choose, *dramatic* would come closer than most. Indeed, looking back from today's vantage point, a larger-than-life quality, almost an epic sweep, defined the period. Bustling commerce, brilliant artistic and other cultural achievements, alliances of city-states, and the clash of major armies and navies all occurred on a scale far larger than Greece had ever before witnessed.

Regarding warfare, some was defensive in nature. The Persian Empire invaded Greece during these years, and many Greeks came together in a concerted effort to drive the intruders away. However, this unity was short-lived. Following the expulsion of the Persians, old rivalries among the Greeks surfaced once more. The most conspicuous rivalry—that between Greece's two leading city-states, Athens and Sparta—steadily escalated into a dangerous contest for supremacy.

Even amid periodic political tensions and bouts of bloodletting and destruction, however, the Greeks channeled some of their amazing energies into more constructive endeavors. In a relatively short time span, Athens witnessed a burst of cultural activity that produced some of the finest architecture, sculpture, and drama ever created. As a result, the mid-to-late fifth century B.C. is today frequently referred to as the golden age of Athens (or of Greece). It is also called the Age of Pericles, in reference to the most influential Athenian leader of that era. Citing Athens's unique attributes and achievements, Pericles predicted with astonishing foresight: "Future ages will wonder at us, as the present age wonders at us now."[9]

The World's First Democracy

Certainly one source of wonder for later generations was Athens's development of the first true democracy the world had ever seen. This new and at the time quite

Artist Peter Connolly depicts a religious procession marching toward an open-air altar atop Athens's Acropolis in the fifth century B.C.

radical political system emerged in 508 B.C. under the influence of an enlightened aristocrat named Cleisthenes. Athens had been moving in the direction of full-blown democracy for some time. Locked in a struggle for popular support with rival nobles, Cleisthenes strongly backed some major democratic reforms and thereby gained the allegiance of a majority of the people. Once the new system was in place, it became self-sustaining and more powerful than any individual leader or group of leaders.

In the fifty to sixty years that followed, the Athenians continued to expand their democracy, making it more open and liberal. Every free male citizen had the right to speak out and vote in the Assembly, which met every ten days or so on the Pnyx Hill (about a third of a mile [0.5km] west of the Acropolis). The members of the Assembly voted to elect the most powerful leaders—the ten *strategoi*, or generals, each of whom would serve a one-year term. The *strategoi* not only commanded the army but carried out the foreign policy formulated by the people.

The people created both foreign and domestic policy through the workings of the Assembly and Council. The latter group, now expanded to five hundred members, drew up legislative bills for the Assembly to discuss and vote on and formed subcommittees to carry out the Assembly's directives. Meanwhile, a number of routine governmental duties were carried out by nine archons, administrators who, like councilmen, were chosen by lot.

Athens's early democracy also featured a radical device designed to prevent one leader from gaining too much power or to sideline a leader whose policies slowed the democratic decision-making process. It was called ostracism. According to scholar Malcolm F. McGregor:

Each [citizen] scratched on a shard [a piece of broken pottery called an ostrakon] the name of the man who

These surviving ostraka from fifth-century B.C. Athens bear the names of politicians earmarked for banishment, including Themistocles.

The Battle of Marathon, 490 B.C.

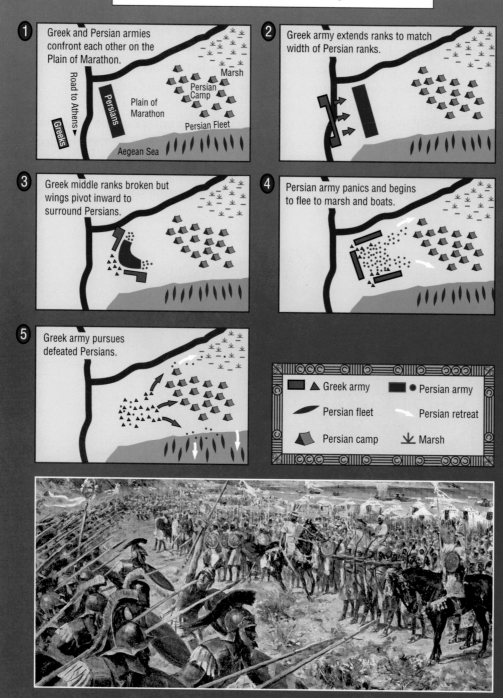

1 Greek and Persian armies confront each other on the Plain of Marathon.

Road to Athens ▶
Greeks
Persians
Plain of Marathon
Persian Camp
Marsh
Persian Fleet
Aegean Sea

2 Greek army extends ranks to match width of Persian ranks.

3 Greek middle ranks broken but wings pivot inward to surround Persians.

4 Persian army panics and begins to flee to marsh and boats.

5 Greek army pursues defeated Persians.

▲ Greek army   ● Persian army

Persian fleet   Persian retreat

Persian camp   ⁘ Marsh

seemed most to threaten [political] stability. . . . He who polled the most votes (6,000 had to be cast) withdrew from [Athens] for ten years without loss of property or citizenship.[10]

Victory at Marathon

No sooner had the Athenians instituted this progressive new form of government when it, their city, and their entire way of life (as well as that of other Greeks) faced the threat of annihilation. A few decades before the start of the Classical Age, most of the Ionian Greek cities had been absorbed into the Persian Empire. Thereafter, the residents of these cities had to pay tribute (money acknowledging submission) to the Persian king and do the bidding of local puppet rulers installed by him. Like other Greek states, the Ionian poleis cherished their independence. So they disliked living under Persian rule and in 499 B.C. they rebelled. The Persian king, Darius I, managed to put down the revolt, but before he did so Athens sent ships and men to aid the rebels. Thereafter, Darius looked forward to exacting revenge on the Athenians for daring to interfere in his affairs. As the fifth-century-B.C. Greek historian Herodotus wrote in his *Histories*, the Persian monarch

asked who the Athenians were, and then, on being told, called for his bow. He took it, set an arrow on the string, shot it up into the air and cried: "Grant,

The diagrams show the major stages of the battle. In the sketch below, the Athenian phalanx nears the Persian ranks.

O God, that I may punish the Athenians." Then he commanded one of his servants to repeat to him the words, "Master, remember the Athenians," three times, whenever he sat down to dinner.[11]

The expedition against Athens occurred in 490 B.C. Though partially punitive in nature, it was also intended as a means of establishing a Persian foothold in Europe. Darius had long dreamed of expanding his realm by conquering large tracts of that continent. The forces he sent, numbering at least twenty thousand fighters, plus an even greater number of sailors and support personnel, landed at Marathon, on the coast of Attica some 26 miles (42km) northeast of Athens.

In response, the Athenians assembled their entire militia of roughly nine thousand men and marched to the plain of Marathon. They were soon joined by about a thousand men from the nearby tiny polis of Plataea, a longtime ally of Athens. At dawn on September 12, the hoplites formed ranks and at a trumpet signal charged at the Persians. "Seeing the attack developing at the double," Herodotus wrote, the Persians thought it was "suicidal madness for the Athenians to risk an assault with so small a force."[12] The display the Persians were witnessing, however, was not one of madness but one of courage and confidence. The heavily armed Greek infantrymen proved vastly superior fighters to the Persian soldiers, who wore little or no armor and were not prepared for the onslaught of the lethal phalanx. Eventually, the Persians fled for their ships. They left behind some 6,400 dead, compared to Athenian losses of only 192 men.

The Second Persian Invasion

All of the Greek city-states celebrated the victory of the hoplites of Marathon, who thereafter became folk heroes. At the same time, many Greeks viewed Athens as Greece's savior and the city gained much prestige. In the decade following the battle at Marathon, the Athenians continued to expand their influence through trade and built a new fleet of warships as well. Clearly, Athens was emerging as the leading naval and economic power in Greece. All this worried the Spartans, who felt that the Athenians were too radical and aggressive and posed a threat to the balance of power in Greece.

Nevertheless, the Spartans and Athenians soon found themselves working together for the mutual survival of all Greeks. After his embarrassing loss at Marathon, Darius vowed to launch another, much larger invasion of Greece. But he died in 485 B.C. Succeeding to the Persian throne, Darius's son, Xerxes (ZERK-seez), determined to resume his father's conquest of Europe. In 480 the new Persian monarch led a huge force, as many as 200,000 troops, across the Hellespont (now the Dardanelles Strait, then separating Asia Minor from the Greek lands). The Persian forces also included an estimated one thousand ships.

Xerxes' plan was to enter southern Greece, where most of the major city-states lay, through the pass of Thermopylae, in the mountains northwest of Boeotia. Leaders of a coalition of Greek states led by Athens and Sparta decided that their best hope of halting the Persian advance was to make a stand at Thermopylae. This was partly because the pass was very narrow. In some places it was only fifty feet wide, Herodotus pointed out, "and the Persians would be unable . . . to use their cavalry or take advantage of their numbers."[13] A small army made up of soldiers from several city-states fortified the pass. They were led by one of Sparta's kings, Leonidas, and three hundred handpicked Spartan hoplites.

The Greeks at Thermopylae managed to hold off the huge enemy army for three days. Aided by their comrades from other cities, the Spartan hoplites slaughtered wave after wave of Persians that Xerxes sent through the pass. In fact, it began to look as though the small band of Greeks might be able to hold the pass indefinitely. But then a Greek traitor led a contingent of Persians along a little-known mountain path toward the Greeks' rear. With only hours to spare, Leonidas ordered most of the Greek soldiers away to safety; then he and a tiny contingent of Spartans and others stayed and fought to the death.

With the pass finally cleared, Xerxes now marched southward unopposed and occupied Athens, which had been largely evacuated in the preceding days. He may have thought that he had finally avenged the wrongs that he believed the Athenians had done his father. But Xerxes' triumph was short-lived. A few days later, a united Greek fleet, led by the Athenian contingent, delivered him a crushing defeat in a battle fought in the straits of Salamis, a few miles west of Athens's urban center. The Athenian play-

In the narrow pass at Thermopylae, the Persians (wearing the pointed helmets) were at first unable to make any headway against the Greeks.

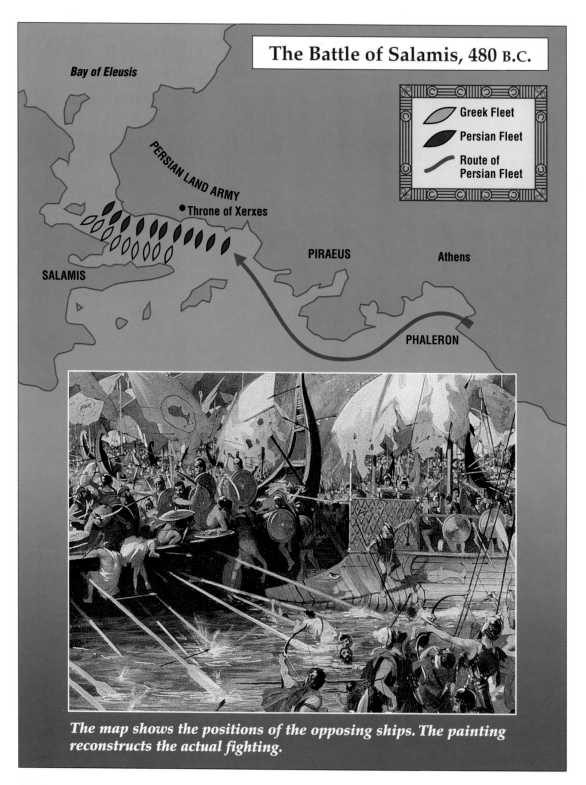

The Battle of Salamis, 480 B.C.

Bay of Eleusis

PERSIAN LAND ARMY

● Throne of Xerxes

SALAMIS

PIRAEUS

Athens

PHALERON

	Greek Fleet
	Persian Fleet
	Route of Persian Fleet

The map shows the positions of the opposing ships. The painting reconstructs the actual fighting.

wright Aeschylus fought in the battle and later, in a play appropriately titled *The Persians*, described the carnage. "Vessels heeled over," he said. So many Persian ships capsized that "the sea was hidden, carpeted with wrecks and dead men; all the shores and reefs were full of dead."[14]

After his loss at Salamis, Xerxes retired to Asia Minor. He left a large portion of his army—perhaps as many as 150,000 men—with orders to invade and destroy the Greek towns that had dared to defy him. But once again he had underestimated Greek abilities and resolve. The following summer (479 B.C.), hoplites from many different Greek states converged on the Persian army, which was camped near

Plataea. Xerxes' troops suffered extremely heavy losses and the survivors fled Greece, never to return.

Greece Divided

The Greeks were proud of their united effort against the Persians. But it did not take long for relations between Athens and Sparta and their respective allies to deteriorate. The late-fifth-century-B.C. Athenian historian Thucydides summed up the new political reality in Greece this way:

> [The Greeks] split into two divisions, one group following Athens and the other Sparta. These were clearly the two most powerful states, one being

Eyewitness to Salamis

The great Athenian playwright Aeschylus presented his play The Persians *in 472 B.C. It contains a passage (here taken from Philip Vellacott's translation) that appears to be an eyewitness account of the battle at Salamis, in which Aeschylus fought. The words are spoken by a Persian messenger to the Persian king's mother.*

A Greek ship charged first and chopped off the whole stern of a Persian galley. Then charge followed charge on every side. At first by its huge impetus our fleet withstood them. But soon, in that narrow space, our ships were jammed in hundreds; none could help another. They rammed each other with their prows of bronze; and some were stripped of every oar. Meanwhile the enemy came round us in a ring and charged. Our vessels heeled over; the sea was hidden, carpeted with wrecks and dead men; all the shores and reefs were full of dead. Then every ship we had broke rank and rowed for life. The Greeks seized fragments of wrecks and broken oars and hacked and stabbed at our men swimming in the sea. . . . The whole sea was one din of shrieks and dying groans, till night and darkness hid the scene.

supreme on land, the other on the sea . . . while among the rest of the Greeks, states that had their own differences now joined one or other of the two sides.[15]

The Spartan alliance was called the Peloponnesian League because most of its members were, like Sparta, located in the Peloponnesus. Athens's alliance—the Delian League—consisted of more than a hundred poleis, many of them scattered across the Aegean and Ionian regions.

At first, the main purpose of the Delian League was to guard against further

The Sources of Pericles' Authority

Modern observers often find it remarkable, even strange, that Pericles was able to wield such potent influence and power in Athens, considering that he was only one of ten elected generals, each of whom, by law, had political authority equal to his. In this excerpt from his biography of Pericles, noted historian Donald Kagan offers an explanation.

Pericles . . . possessed no great private fortune . . . no military or police forces, and he could expend no public money without a vote of the popular assembly of citizens. . . . Each year he had to stand for reelection and was constantly subject to public scrutiny and political challenge. . . . [His influence derived from] . . . the power of his ideas, the strength of his personality, the use of reason, and his genius as a uniquely persuasive [public speaker]. In ancient Athens, the people decided policy in oral debate in the open air. Skill in public speaking was essential, and Pericles was the greatest orator of his day by common consent.

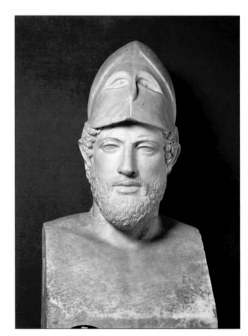

This bust of the Athenian statesman Pericles is presently on display at a museum in Vatican City in Rome.

This reconstructed bird's eye view shows the Long Walls stretching from Athens's urban center to its port town of Piraeus (seen in inset).

attacks by the Persians and, when possible, to disrupt Persian activities in Asia Minor. But over time, these goals became secondary to those of Athens, the leading state in the alliance. As Thucydides wrote, the Athenians used their extensive naval power to control and sometimes even bully their own allies, in the process turning the league into a virtual Athenian empire:

> The Athenians insisted on obligations being exactly met, and made themselves unpopular by bringing the severest pressure to bear on allies who were not used to making sacrifices and did not want to make them. . . . [The Athenians forced] back into the alliance any state that wanted to leave it. The result was that the Athenian navy grew strong at [the allies'] expense.[16]

The Rise of Pericles

The Spartans watched the growth of Athens's power with a great deal of trepidation. They were particularly bothered by events that occurred shortly after Pericles came to power as Athens's most influential general in 462 B.C. Pericles was an ardent champion of democracy, a system the Spartans viewed as unstable and a major cause of Athens's aggressive foreign policy. He was also staunchly anti-Spartan and was not afraid to provoke Athens's traditional rival.

Pericles on Citizen Participation in Government

One thing that bothered the Spartans about Pericles was his advocacy of the concept of radical democracy, in which common people of all walks of life took part in political debate and lawmaking. In his Peloponnesian War, *Thucydides quoted Pericles as saying:*

As for poverty, no one need be ashamed to admit it. The real shame is not taking practical measures to escape from it. Here, each individual is interested not only in his own affairs but in the affairs of state as well. Even those who are mostly occupied with their own business are extremely well informed on general politics. This is a peculiarity of ours. We do not say that a man who takes no interest in politics is a man who minds his own business. We say that he has no business here at all.

One of the most serious Athenian provocations, from Sparta's point of view, was the erection of the Long Walls in 458 B.C. Pericles felt that Athens's existing defenses were inadequate to stop a Spartan invasion and also that the landlocked Athenian urban center needed a more effective way to tap into its naval lifeline at its port town, Piraeus. To meet these needs, Pericles convinced the people to construct the Long Walls, a defensive perimeter stretching the entire four miles from the urban center to Piraeus.

This did more than make Athens a formidable fortress that could be supplied by sea on an unlimited basis. The many lower-class laborers and sailors who lived and worked in the port area now felt more connected to the urban center and began playing a bigger role in city politics. In turn, this increased participation by ordinary citizens made the Assembly more democratic and responsive to the people's needs. Other democratic reforms followed, including a bill Pericles pushed through that provided pay for jurors. Now, poor people could afford to take time away from work to serve the state.

These and other developments motivated the notoriously cautious Spartans to act. They assembled an army made up partly of their own hoplites and partly of soldiers from their allies in the Peloponnesus and elsewhere. In 457 B.C. the Athenians, reinforced by some of their own allies, met them in battle at Tanagra (near Thebes). The immediate outcome was largely indecisive. But this relatively minor clash of arms foreshadowed far more destructive conflict to come. As the Athenians and others enjoyed prosperity and erected magnificent temples and other structures, what Thucydides called "the greatest disturbance in the history of the Greeks"[17] began to take shape on the horizon.

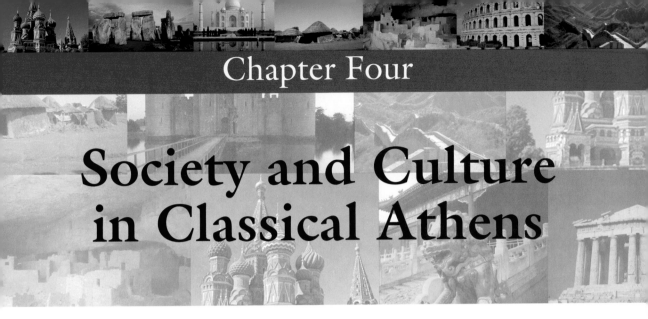

Chapter Four

Society and Culture in Classical Athens

Unfortunately, much of the evidence for social customs and cultural endeavors in most Greek city-states during the Classical Age has disappeared over the centuries. The major exception is Athens. Indeed, most of the surviving first-hand information about Greek civilization comes from Athenian writers and describes Athenian history, customs, and ideas. Athens was the largest, most populous, and most prosperous Greek polis, so it was not by any means average as Greek city-states went. Nevertheless, scholars believe that examining life in classical Athens fairly represents what life was like in most other parts of Greece in this period. (An obvious exception was Sparta, with its rigid military customs and conservative political ideas.)

In the area of arts and culture, by contrast, Athens was truly exceptional. In its so-called golden age (or Age of Pericles), its architects, artisans, and writers produced a burst of creative activity that con-

tinues to astonish people today. The incredible scope and speed of this achievement was attributable to the fact that the Athenians enjoyed a unique set of circumstances. First, Athens was a major center of commerce and knowledge. A constant influx of goods and ideas from the far corners of the Mediterranean world made it a highly cosmopolitan, or worldly, city. The Athenians also accumulated a huge amount of wealth, partly from trade and partly from their rich silver mines in southern Attica. In addition, the city's democratic institutions greatly encouraged individual expression. A combination of these and other factors made Athens a modern, progressive, and tolerant place; it attracted artisans and thinkers from across the Greek world and beyond.

Metics and Slaves

Many of the artists, builders, writers, and others who made Athens great were free males who were citizens because they

Athenian Slaves: Too Well Treated?

Some older, more conservative Athenians found it irritating that domestic slaves were often so well treated and protected by antiabuse laws. An anonymous late-fifth-century-B.C. writer explained this sentiment in a document translated in Xenophon's Scripta Minora.

Among the slaves and metics at Athens there is the greatest uncontrolled wantonness. You can't hit them there, and a slave will not stand aside for you [when you meet him in the street]. . . . If it were customary for a slave . . . to be struck by one who is free, you would often hit an Athenian citizen by mistake on the assumption that he was a slave. For the people there are no better dressed than slaves and metics.

This rendering is based on a sixth-century B.C. Athenian vase painting of a slave carrying storage containers called amphorae.

were born in the city. Women born in Athens were citizens, too. However, they belonged to a special class of citizen that lacked political rights. Free noncitizen men and women and slaves of both genders also contributed time, labor, and talent to the city's rise to wealth and glory. Without the efforts of these groups, Athens's more famous creative elite could not have accomplished what they did.

Free Athenians who lacked citizenship because they were born in other Greek cities or foreign lands were called metics. Most often they were traders and craftspeople who came to live and work in Athens. Although they could not attend the Assembly or take part in other governmental affairs, many metics became prosperous, respected members of the community. They provided many vital services and sometimes fought in the army.

Athenian citizens also benefited from the services and support of slaves, who did most of the menial work in homes and much of the unskilled labor on public building projects. Most slaves were captured in wars or bought from slave traders, although a few were bred in the home. Modern estimates for the number of Athenian slaves vary, but roughly a third of Attica's quarter of a million people in the fifth century B.C. likely lived in servitude.

A few Athenians apparently thought that the idea of one person owning another was wrong. The playwright Euripides, for example, wrote: "How wretched a thing slavery is, forcing the weak to endure the ill treatment of the strong."[18] However, the vast majority of Athenians, like other people in the ancient world, accepted slavery as a natural and necessary institution.

Yet unlike slave owners in most other places and times, on the whole the Athenians treated their slaves humanely. Those slaves that worked in the city's silver mines were shackled and suffered badly. But domestic slaves were usually well treated, and the law protected household slaves from severe abuse. A free person who beat or killed another person's slave could be prosecuted, for example. Also, it was illegal for an owner to kill his own slave, no matter what crime the slave committed.

Athenian Women

Athenian women, wealthy and poor alike, also contributed to the city's prosperity by performing many essential duties. Among the more important were child rearing, housekeeping, and fabric and clothes making. Women also cooked, did laundry, and often paid the household bills.

By modern standards, Athenian women led sheltered, restricted lives. They could not take part in politics and were expected to obey their fathers and husbands at all times. A majority of women were also confined to the home most of the time, and when they did go out (to attend the theater, for instance), they had to be accompanied by a male relative or slave. Also, when the head of the household entertained male friends, his wife, daughters, mother, and/or sisters had to retire to the "women's quarters" (*gynaeceum*), located in the back of the house or upstairs. The main reason for such rules was that husbands and fathers were very concerned about their wives' and daughters' chastity and marital fidelity. So it was seen as essential to keep the family women from associating with unrelated men, who might corrupt them and thereby destabilize the family.

Eventually, however, a father (or other male relative) arranged for his daughters to marry nonfamilial men of his own choosing. Following custom, most Athenian women married when they were in their early to midteens, while men often waited till they were close to thirty to tie the knot. No detailed written descriptions of an ancient Greek wedding have survived. However, Sue Blundell, an authority on ancient Greek women, has pieced together a credible scenario from various literary and visual sources:

This nineteenth-century woodcut depicts women performing various tasks in the women's quarters of a greek house.

The public part of the ceremony began with a wedding feast in the house of the bride's father. At nightfall, the partially veiled bride, the groom, and the groom's best friend were carried to the couple's future home in a nuptial chariot drawn by mules, accompanied by a torchlit procession of friends and relatives singing nuptial hymns. . . . At their destination the bride was greeted by her mother-in-law, who was carrying torches, and was formally conducted to the hearth, the focal point of her new home. Meanwhile, bride and groom were showered with nuts and dried fruits, emblems of fertility and prosperity. . . . The climax of the proceedings came when the bride was led by the groom towards the bridal chamber, while a wedding hymn was sung by the guests.[19]

Educating Young Men

Because women usually did not take part in government or produce art or literature, they received no formal education. Most of the time, mothers taught their daughters the household arts at home. Many young men, on the other hand, received fairly extensive schooling, especially in the later years of the Classical Age. Most Athenian boys began attending school at about age seven or eight. The schools were privately run and paid for mostly by parents. (The government paid for the education of boys whose fathers had died in battle defending the community.) Instructors called *grammatistes* taught boys reading and writing.

Having learned to read, young men began studying the works of poets, especially Homer. The Greeks came to view his texts as vital sources of literary, artistic, moral, social, educational, and political instruction, as well as practical wisdom. "In Homer," scholar Robert Flaceliere remarks, "was contained whatever knowledge a man worthy of his name could need."[20] Schoolboys also learned to sing and play the lyre (a small harp) from music teachers known as *kitharistes*, and practiced dancing and athletic events with gym instructors called *paidotribes*.

At age eighteen, most Athenian youths received another form of schooling—basic military training. It included instruction in fighting with spears and swords and working in concert with fellow soldiers in the phalanx. When the training was completed, the recruits, called *ephebes*, recited the following oath:

I will not bring dishonor on my sacred arms nor will I abandon my comrade wherever I shall be stationed. I will defend the rights of gods and men and will not leave my country smaller, when I die, but greater and better, so far as I am able by myself and with the help of all. I will respect the rulers of the time duly and the existing ordinances duly and all others which may be established in the future. And if anyone seeks to destroy the ordinances I will oppose him so far as I am able by myself and with the help of all.[21]

A painting from an ancient Greek vase shows a young woman's relatives leading her to meet the man chosen to be her husband.

These school scenes painted on a fifth-century B.C. cup show students writing and playing instruments as their teachers look on.

The Acropolis and Parthenon

The Athenian people took great pride in those young men who became well-rounded individuals displaying a combination of physical and intellectual excellence. All of Athens's inhabitants, whether male or female, free or slave, were also proud of its architectural and artistic achievements, which were unrivaled in Greece at the time. The government used much of the city's wealth, including tribute collected from members of the Delian League, to erect new public buildings.

The culmination of these efforts began in the 440s B.C. when Pericles initiated an ambitious construction program for the Acropolis. The summit of the hill was eventually transformed into a magnificent complex of temples, shrines, gateways, statues, and altars. Thousands of Athenians of all walks of life took part, as Plutarch recalled in his biography of Pericles:

The materials to be used were stone, bronze, ivory, gold, ebony, and cypress-wood, while the arts or trades which wrought or fashioned them were those of carpenter, modeler, coppersmith, stone-mason, dyer, worker in gold and ivory, painter, embroiderer, and engraver, and besides these the carriers and suppliers of the materials, such as merchants, sailors, and pilots for the sea-borne traffic, and wagon-makers, trainers of draft-animals, and drivers for everything that came by land. There

Phidias's Great Statue of Athena

Phidias's colossal statue inside the Parthenon—the Athena Parthenos—*was one of the wonders of the ancient world. The second-century-*A.D. *Greek traveler Pausanias described it in his famous guidebook to Greek sites.*

As you go into the temple, [you can see that] the statue is made of ivory and gold. She [Athena] has a sphinx on the middle of her helmet, and griffins worked on either side of it. . . . The griffins are wild monsters like lions with wings and the beak of an eagle. . . . The statue of Athena stands upright in an ankle-length tunic with the head of Medusa [a mythical monster] carved in ivory on her breast[plate]. She [Athena] has a [statue of the goddess] Victory about eight feet high [in one hand] and a spear in her [other] hand, and a shield at her feet, and a snake beside the shield.

This modern painting of Phidias's statue of Athena is based on the eyewitness description Pausanias gave in his guidebook.

Modern restorations of the Parthenon show its magnificent exterior and the structural elements of the interior.

Within one wing of the Propylaea, the Acropolis's monumental gateway, was an art gallery (right).

In this modern painting, Phidias shows invited guests the Parthenon's still unfinished frieze of sculpted figures.

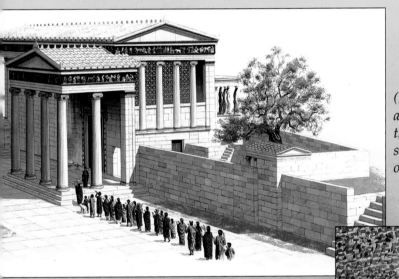

Sculptures from the Parthenon are shown both in the their present ruined state and as they originally looked (left and above).

(Left) Athenian citizens approach the north portal of the Erechtheum, a temple situated near the Parthenon on the Acropolis.

A painted aerial view shows the Athenian Acropolis as it appeared in its original glory.

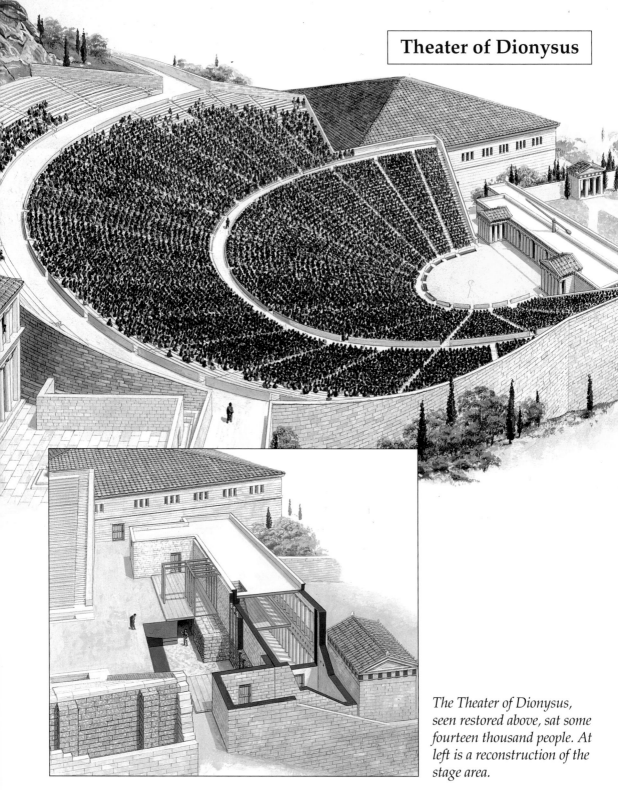

The Theater of Dionysus, seen restored above, sat some fourteen thousand people. At left is a reconstruction of the stage area.

were also rope-makers, weavers, leatherworkers, road-builders, and miners. Each individual craft, like a general with an army under his separate command, had its own corps of unskilled laborers at its disposal . . . [and consequently] the city's prosperity was extended far and wide and shared among every age and condition in Athens.[22]

The largest and most splendid structure atop the Acropolis was the Parthenon, dedicated to Athens's patron deity, Athena (goddess of war and wisdom). It was designed by the architect Ictinus and decorated by Phidias, now recognized as the greatest sculptor of the ancient world. Measuring 237 feet (72m) long, 110 feet (33.5m) wide, and 60 feet (18m) high, the building contained more than 22,000 tons (19,958 metric tons) of marble. Inside stood Phidias's dazzling 40-foot-tall (12m) statue of the goddess. It was made of wood, ivory, and some 2,500 pounds (1,134kg) of pure gold. So impressive was the Parthenon that an early modern visitor to Athens was moved to remark: "All the world's culture culminated in Greece, all Greece in Athens, all Athens in its Acropolis, all the Acropolis in the Parthenon."[23]

Attending the Theater

The theater was another example of Athenian creativity, ambition, and sheer talent. In a sense, Athens invented and perfected this now familiar literary and artistic institution overnight. In less than a century, a series of informal songs and speeches recited by worshippers in road-side religious processions evolved into formal dramatic competitions held in large public facilities. Almost all of the theatrical concepts familiar today, including tragedy, comedy, acting, directing, costumes, scenery, and even theater tickets and acting awards, originated in Athens in the sixth and fifth centuries B.C.

Beginning in the 490s B.C., plays were presented in the Theater of Dionysus, nestled near the base of the Acropolis. The dramatic competitions were part of the City Dionysia, a religious festival held in March in honor of the fertility god Dionysus. Admission was free at first, but increasing demand for seats soon necessitated the introduction of tickets (in about 450 B.C. by Pericles). These took the form of tokens that looked similar to coins and were made of bronze, lead, ivory, bone, or terra-cotta (baked clay).

Over the course of a few days, several playwrights presented their works, which at first were exclusively tragedies. The stories came mostly from mythology and explored the relationship between people and gods, as well as basic human emotions and social and moral themes of interest to all. When comedy was introduced in the early fifth century B.C., it provided audiences with an emotional release and relief from the grimness of the tragic presentations. The comic plays also became an important outlet for political expression by poking fun, often with unheard-of candor, at community institutions and leaders.

An Education to Greece

It was this very openness, irreverence, and sheer audacity that made many other

The Theater of Dionysus

The first Athenian theater was erected perhaps in the early 530s B.C. Its exact location and physical layout are unknown. But evidence suggests that it consisted of a circular "dancing place," or orchestra, where the actors performed, and an audience area (*theatron*) with wooden bleachers. About 499 B.C. these seats collapsed in the middle of a performance, killing many of the spectators.

Soon afterward, the Athenians constructed the Theater of Dionysus against the southeastern base of the Acropolis. In its initial form, the theater featured an orchestra 85 feet (26m) in diameter. To avoid another disaster, the seating, which could accommodate up to fourteen thousand spectators, consisted of wooden planking covering earthen tiers carved into the hillside. (In a fourth-century-B.C. renovation, the wooden seats were replaced by stone versions.) A rectangular structure called the *skene*, or "scene building," was erected behind the orchestra facing the audience. The *skene* provided a background for the actors and also housed dressing rooms and perhaps a storage area for stage props.

Greeks uncomfortable. At the same time that they built their splendid temples and flocked to the theater, the Athenians continued to dominate their allies and provoke their adversaries. Indeed, they did so with an air of confidence, even of superiority. Pericles summed up the prevailing Athenian view of the city's preeminent place in Greek affairs, saying:

> There is a great contrast between us and most other people. . . . I declare that our city is an education to Greece. . . . To show that this is no empty boasting . . . you have only to consider the power which our city possesses. . . . Athens, alone of the states we know, comes to her testing time in a greatness that surpasses what was imagined of her. . . . Mighty indeed are the marks and monuments of our empire.[24]

Needless to say, this rather arrogant attitude did not endear Pericles and his countrymen to the Spartans. Some Greeks worried that sooner or later Sparta and its own allies would feel compelled to contain Athens's arrogance and aggressive foreign policy. And if so, there might be no way to avoid a terrible ordeal of total war.

Chapter Five

Incessant Warfare Exhausts the Greeks

It was perhaps inevitable that the two strongest Greek powers—Athens and Sparta—would eventually fight each other. Each was convinced that it alone should enjoy supremacy in Greece. And after decades of tensions, mistrust, and rivalry between these cities, each finally reached a point where it was willing to fight a major war to gain that supremacy.

The conflict—which became known as the Peloponnesian War—did not affect only these powerful cities, however. Each drew in its respective allies, widening the conflict until it engulfed nearly all of the Greek city-states. "I saw, too, that the rest of the Greek world was committed to one side or the other," Thucydides reported in his masterful chronicle of the war. The conflict also affected "a large part of the non-Greek world," he added, "and indeed, I might also say, the whole of mankind."[25] In fact, the war did end up being the equivalent of a modern world war to the Greeks. It lasted a grueling twenty-seven

years, caused widespread death and misery, and exhausted the resources and energies of all involved.

Perhaps an even worse consequence of what many Greeks called the "great war" was that those who had waged it did not learn its most important lesson: that the continued disunity of the Greek states was futile and only served to weaken them all. The result was that the fourth century B.C., roughly encompassing the second half of the Classical Age, proved to be a period of further fighting and war weariness. A succession of states each achieved momentary success and the hegemony, or dominance, of Greece. But none was able to exploit the situation for long, and all Greeks eventually found themselves caught in a downward spiral of political and military decline.

Causes of the Great War

Before the outbreak of the Peloponnesian War, Athens and Sparta more or less

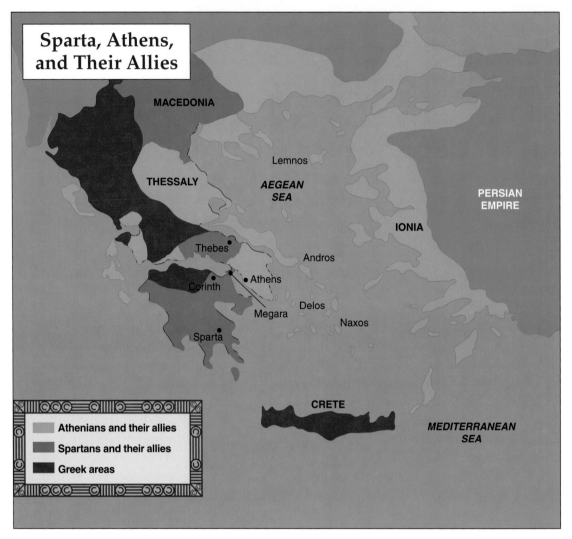

 is placeholder — the map appears at the top of the page with the following labels:

Sparta, Athens, and Their Allies

MACEDONIA

THESSALY

Lemnos

AEGEAN SEA

PERSIAN EMPIRE

IONIA

Thebes

Andros

Corinth

Athens

Megara

Delos

Naxos

Sparta

CRETE

MEDITERRANEAN SEA

Athenians and their allies

Spartans and their allies

Greek areas

shared the hegemony of Greece. Each, of course, hoped to increase its own influence in Greek affairs at the expense of the other. And the constant mutual distrust and rivalry of these states was the main long-term cause of the war.

One of the more immediate causes of the conflict involved one of Sparta's major Peloponnesian allies, Corinth, and Corcyra, an island polis that Corinth had colonized centuries before. In 435 B.C. Corinth and Corcyra got into a serious dis-

pute over one of Corcyra's own colonies, a city called Epidamnus. A sea battle ensued, which the Corinthians lost. But Corinth, long a major sea power in the region, rapidly built a new and even larger fleet, which greatly worried the Corcyreans. In 433 they appealed to Athens to protect them. After some debate, the Athenian Assembly decided to send ten ships to aid Corcyra. Meanwhile, Corinth dispatched 150 warships to Corcyrean waters, and there another sea battle took place, in which the Corcyreans and Athenians squared off against the Corinthians. Once more, Corinth was forced to withdraw.

The enraged Corinthians now appealed to Sparta, asking that it mobilize its much feared army and punish the meddlesome Athenians. Berating Spartan leaders for their slowness to act against Athens, the Corinthian envoys said:

> Many times before now we told you what we were likely to suffer from Athens, and on each occasion, instead

Military Training in Sparta

One major reason the Spartans were able to develop such an effective and feared army was that they instituted a highly regimented military training system (the agoge*). Spartan elders examined all male infants and ordered those they saw as too weak to be exposed, or left outside to die. Spartan boys who were allowed to live entered state-run schools at age seven. Although they received instruction in basic reading and writing, poetry, and patriotic songs, the emphasis was on physical endurance and military training. Plutarch explained this system in his* Life of Lycurgus *(translated by Richard J.A. Talbert in* Plutarch on Sparta*).*

Their whole education was aimed at developing smart obedience, perseverance under stress, and victory in battle. So as they grew older, they intensified their physical training, and got into the habit of cropping their hair, going barefoot, and exercising naked. From the age of twelve, they never wore a tunic, and were given only one cloak a year. . . . They slept together . . . on mattresses which they made for themselves from the tips of [river] reeds.

A modern drawing shows young Spartan men training.

of taking to heart what we were telling you, you chose instead . . . to consider that we were speaking only about our own grievances. . . . You can see yourselves how Athens has deprived some states of their freedom and is scheming to do the same for others . . . and that she herself has for a long time been preparing for the eventuality of war. . . . And it is you [i.e., the Spartans] who are responsible for all this. It was you who in the first place allowed the Athenians to fortify their city and build the Long Walls after the Persian War.[26]

The Plague's Debilitating Symptoms

This is part of the detailed description Thucydides gave in his great war chronicle of the symptoms of the plague that struck Athens in 430 B.C.

People in perfect health suddenly began to have burning feelings in the head. Their eyes became red and inflamed. Inside their mouths there was bleeding from the throat and tongue, and the breath became unnatural and unpleasant. . . . Before long, the pain settled on the chest and was accompanied by coughing. Next the stomach was affected, with stomach-aches and with vomiting. . . . The skin was rather reddish and livid, breaking out into small pustules [boils] and ulcers. . . . If people survived this critical period, then the disease descended into the bowels, producing violent . . . and uncontrollable diarrhea, so that most of them died later as a result of the weakness caused by this. It affected the genitals, fingers, and toes, and many of those who recovered lost the use of these members. Some, too, went blind.

A Greek doctor tries to help victims of an epidemic.

Despite these strong words, the Spartans still refused to act. Pericles and other Athenian leaders were relieved. They were also emboldened to put on a show of force, a move designed to send a warning to Corinth that it should refrain from retaliating against either Athens or Corcyra. The city-state of Megara, a Spartan ally lying just west of Athens, had recently declared its support for Corinth. So Athens now imposed a total trade embargo on Megara. Unable to import enough food to sustain themselves, the Megarians faced the threat of starvation. This was too much for the Spartans. Finally deciding that Athens had gone too far, they declared war in 431 B.C.

Destruction and Disease Take a Toll

At first, the combatants adopted highly contrasting strategies. Sparta planned a conventional approach—attacking Attica by land, burning its houses, and laying waste to the countryside. The Spartans reasoned that this would disrupt agriculture and spread fear and chaos through the region. Hopefully the demoralized Athenians would quickly surrender.

Athens's strategy, on the other hand, was decidedly *un*conventional. Pericles and his fellow generals realized from the outset that marching out and confronting the fearsome Spartan phalanx would be foolhardy. So they convinced their fellow citizens to adopt a more defensive approach, one that took advantage of the Long Walls and the city's extensive fleets. The entire population of Attica would take refuge behind the walls. They would then rely on their cargo ships to keep them well supplied and on their warships to harass enemy trade and attack the coasts of the Peloponnesus. Eventually, Pericles argued, the Spartans would grow tired and frustrated and give up the fight.

Each side proceeded to put its plan into action. In the summer of 431 B.C. the Spartans marched into Attica and burned Athenian homes and farms. But this accomplished little because Athens still retained complete control of the seas. Without significant opposition, Athenian warships laid waste to Peloponnesian coastal towns. The following year, both sides implemented the same strategy and it appeared that the war might turn into a standoff.

However, this time the Athenians had to deal with an unexpected enemy. A terrible plague struck their city, spreading with frightening swiftness through the crowded shantytowns that had been erected inside the Long Walls. Thucydides, who contracted the disease himself but survived, later described some of the initial symptoms:

> [People's] eyes became red and inflamed. Inside their mouths there was bleeding from the throat and tongue, and the breath became unnatural and unpleasant. . . . The skin was rather reddish . . . breaking out into small pustules and ulcers. But inside there was a feeling of burning.[27]

The effects of the plague were devastating. In only a few months at least 20 percent of the city's population died. To make matters worse, the disease struck down Pericles, who succumbed in 429 B.C.

With the city's strongest leader gone, two factions vied to fill the power vacuum he had left. One, led by a politician named Cleon, wanted to keep fighting until Athens attained a clear victory. The other faction, led by a wealthy citizen named

This marble bust of the notorious traitor Alcibiades is on display in Florence, Italy.

Nicias, favored making peace with Sparta. At first, the Assembly followed Cleon's policy. But after seven more years of relentless death and destruction, the Athenians came around to the other view. In the late 420s Nicias brokered a treaty, which became known as the Peace of Nicias in his honor.

Double Disaster for Athens

As it happened, however, the treaty never took full effect. This was partly because some of Sparta's major allies, notably Corinth and Thebes, refused to acknowledge it. They wanted no part of peace until Athens was defeated and humbled.

Meanwhile, on the opposing side, a new war leader came to power in Athens—Alcibiades, foster son of Pericles and one of the most colorful characters the city ever produced. Alcibiades was brilliant and audacious on the one hand and arrogant and unprincipled on the other. Hoping to revive the war against a weakened Sparta, he persuaded some of Sparta's allies to rebel. Part of this strategy worked, as Sparta resumed the fight against Athens, but part backfired, as the Spartans handily defeated the rebels and remained as strong as ever.

Alcibiades now hatched a daring scheme, one that many Athenians, including Nicias, viewed as foolhardy. Alcibiades proposed that Athens amass a huge force of warships and soldiers and attack the Greek city of Syracuse, in Sicily. Supposedly, this would give

Spartan ships enter the harbor at Piraeus following their major defeat of an Athenian war fleet. Athens had no choice but to surrender.

Athens control of all of Sicily, including its abundant foodstuffs and human resources; the Athenians would then easily be able to defeat the Peloponnesian League. Though the venture was clearly risky, the Assembly went along with it. And Athens ended up paying a heavy price. The Sicilian expedition, launched in 415 B.C., failed utterly, resulting in the loss of more than a hundred ships and some forty thousand men. As Thucydides later grimly and concisely summed it up, the "losses were, as they say, total; army, navy, everything was destroyed."[28]

Though devastated by the disaster at Syracuse, the Athenians endeavored to continue the war. But they never fully recovered. And the advantage in the conflict steadily shifted toward the Spartan-led alliance. Sparta set up permanent forts in Attica, forcing the Athenians to hide behind the Long Walls year-round. The Spartans also made an alliance with Greece's former enemy, Persia, which supplied the money for the Spartans, traditionally land-lubbers, to build a war fleet of their own.

This proved to be the strategic turning point. In 405 B.C. the new Spartan navy decisively defeated an Athenian fleet in the northern Aegean, and the following year Athens surrendered. The victors forced the vanquished to tear down the Long Walls and temporarily abolished Athens's cherished democracy. The city's proud golden age was over.

The Spartan Hegemony

But Athens was not the only city that had been damaged by the war. The conflict had killed tens of thousands of people, devastated hundreds of towns and cities, and deepened traditional mutual resentments and disunities among the city-states. In some ways, all of Greece emerged weaker, less stable, and less certain about the future than ever before.

At first, because of its victory over Athens, Sparta dominated Greek affairs. But the Spartans failed to maintain their hegemony, partly because they were not able administrators. They were also insensitive and heavy-handed in their dealings with other Greeks, including their own allies. For example, in 382 B.C. Sparta turned on Thebes, an ally during the great war. Spartan hoplites occupied the Theban acropolis in support of a local antidemocratic, pro-Spartan coup. During the first three decades of the fourth century B.C., such Spartan bully tactics provoked a series of small wars between Sparta and various other city-states. These conflicts further exhausted the already war-weary Greek cities. Meanwhile, Athens responded to what it viewed as overt Spartan aggressions by building up another bloc of its own allies.

The Rise of Thebes

It was not Athens, however, that ended the Spartan hegemony. In the 370s B.C., shortly after the Spartan occupation of Thebes began, a patriotic politician and brilliant military innovator named Epaminondas rose to prominence in that city. Aided by another Theban patriot, Pelopidas, he overhauled the city's military. Pelopidas drilled the Sacred Band, a unit of three hundred elite fighters, each of whom was a match for the best Spartan hoplite. In the meantime, Epaminondas taught the soldiers in the main army some new and unusual battlefield tactics.

These tactics were based on Epaminondas's careful observations of the traditional way that Greek generals arranged their infantry. He noted that they almost always placed their best troops on the right wing of the phalanx. When two opposing armies met, the strong right wings always faced weaker enemy left wings. Thus, the army with the most powerful right wing was usually able to crush the opposing left wing and then outflank, or move around and behind, the other army, assuring victory. In the words of noted military historian Peter Connolly:

Epaminondas believed that if he could knock out the crack Spartan troops on the right wing, the rest of the Spartan army would collapse. In order to achieve this, he planned to reverse his battle order, placing his own weakest troops on the right, opposite the Spartan left, lining up the phalanx *en echelon* [obliquely, or at an angle], with the weakest troops held back, whilst at the same time massing his best troops on the left, supported by the strongest cavalry and the Sacred Band.[29]

To give his left wing even more power, Epaminondas made it fifty rows deep, as compared to the twelve rows of the Spartan left wing.

The fateful battle that tested these new tactics occurred in July 371 B.C. near Leuctra, a village ten miles southwest of Thebes. Epaminondas's plan succeeded with brutal efficiency. A thousand Spartans, including their king, were slain, while the Thebans and their Boeotian allies lost just forty-seven men. In a single, dramatic stroke, Epaminondas had dispelled the myth of Spartan invincibility and raised Thebes to the dominant position in Greece.

The Theban Hegemony

Sparta's unexpected defeat immediately changed the political climate of Greece,

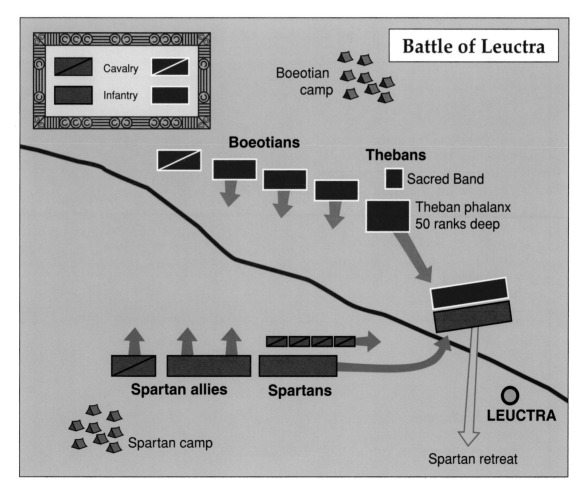

Battle of Leuctra

Cavalry

Infantry

Boeotian camp

Boeotians

Thebans

Sacred Band

Theban phalanx 50 ranks deep

Spartan allies

Spartans

Spartan camp

LEUCTRA

Spartan retreat

especially in the Peloponnesus. Supported by Thebes, most of the Peloponnesian cities that had long followed Sparta out of fear threw out their Spartan-backed oligarchies and proclaimed independence. (Most instituted some form of democracy.) The leading towns of Arcadia, the region encompassing the central Peloponnesus, formed a confederacy. And less than a year after Leuctra, with Epaminondas's aid, they

Epaminondas's Daughters

The Greek historian Diodorus Siculus gave this account (translated in volume seven of his Library of History) *of Epaminondas's death following the struggle at Mantinea.*

When [the Spartans] saw that Epaminondas in the fury of battle was pressing forward too eagerly, they charged [at] him. . . . As the missiles flew thick and fast around him . . . he received a mortal wound in the chest. . . . About his body a rivalry ensued in which many were slain on both sides. . . . [Later, in his camp] physicians were summoned. . . . They declared that . . . as soon as the spearpoint should be drawn from his chest, death would ensue. . . . [He asked] which side was victorious [and hearing it was his own] directed them to withdraw the spear-point. [One of his friends cried out] "You die childless, Epaminondas," and burst into tears. To this he replied, "No, by Zeus, on the contrary, I leave behind two daughters, Leuctra and Mantinea, my victories."

Epaminondas confronts the oncoming enemy at Mantinea. He died shortly after the battle.

established a central capital, calling it Megalopolis ("great city").

In the following few years, Epaminondas and his troops performed several of what amounted to police actions in the Peloponnesus and other parts of Greece. Their intentions were usually good. They were dismayed, therefore, to find that it was impossible to maintain political balance and stability in Greece without angering or alienating one state or another. Athens remained openly hostile to the Theban hegemony, for instance. And relations between Thebes and the Arcadian confederacy became increasingly strained.

The last police action Epaminondas felt compelled to take in the Peloponnesus occurred in 362 B.C. Open warfare broke out between some of the Arcadian cities and their neighbor, Elis. Then, itching to reassert its authority in the region, Sparta became involved, and the Thebans saw no other choice but armed intervention. Reaching Mantinea (north of Megalopolis)

in late summer, Epaminondas's army faced a powerful coalition of hoplites from Sparta, Athens, and various Peloponnesian cities. The battle that ensued was the largest ever fought by Greeks against Greeks up to that time, involving more than fifty thousand combatants in all. It ended more or less in a draw. Xenophon, whose two sons took part in the fight, said later that now "there was even more uncertainty and confusion in Greece . . . than there had been previously."[30]

Part of this uncertainty derived from the fact that Epaminondas was wounded in the battle and died shortly afterward. Without his strong leadership, Thebes was no longer able to maintain its dominance in Greek affairs. For the moment, the major Greek cities, exhausted from years of strife, settled into an uneasy truce. They had no way of knowing that soon they would all face a new and powerful enemy, one who would take full advantage of their disunity and exhaustion.

Chapter Six

The Conquests of Philip and Alexander

The Peloponnesian War and the smaller conflicts that followed it in the early fourth century B.C. took their toll on the Greek city-states. Weakened and vulnerable to outside attack, they were ill prepared for the emergence of a formidable new military power in their own backyard. In the middle of the fourth century B.C., the feuding tribes of Macedonia, in extreme northern Greece, united into a strong kingdom. The city-state Greeks, especially in the cultured cities of the southern mainland, had long viewed Macedonia as a primitive cultural backwater. As noted classical scholar Peter Green colorfully puts it:

> They regarded Macedonians in general as semi-savages, uncouth of speech and dialect, retrograde in their political institutions, negligible as fighters, and habitual oath-breakers, who dressed in bear pelts and were much given to . . . [drunkenness], tempered

with regular bouts of assassination and incest.[31]

The result of this contemptuous attitude was that most Greeks largely ignored Macedonia as it amassed a powerful military force. This was a grave mistake. Under their brilliant king and war leader, Philip II, the Macedonians proved themselves more than a match for the best fighters the city-states could muster. Philip succeeded in ending the long age of autonomous, warring city-states. And his equally talented son, Alexander III (later called "the Great"), led the Greeks in conquests that spread Greek culture and ideas across much of the known world.

A Quest for Power and Culture

The rise of Macedonia as a great power began when Philip ascended to the throne in 359 B.C. At the time, many Macedonians belonged to fiercely independent hill tribes and the country was disorganized and weak. Wanting to remedy this situation, Philip set about unifying the tribes. His principal tool was the creation of Europe's first national, professional standing army. In contrast to the militias utilized by the city-states, which were called up only when needed, Philip's army was a large permanent force whose members received extensive training. Philip also paid them handsome rewards, including parcels of land and the spoils gained in their victories. These incentives motivated thousands of young men from all over Macedonia to join Philip's new national organization.

Part of what made the Macedonian army effective was Philip's reorganization and improvement of the traditional Greek phalanx. He armed his troops with long pikes (*sarrisas*), the points of which projected from the front of the formation in a frightening mass of metal. Neither regular foot soldiers nor cavalry (mounted fighters) had a chance of penetrating the Macedonian phalanx.

After unifying Macedonia, Philip gazed with envious eyes on Athens and the other splendid cultural centers of southern Greece. He planned to take advantage of their weakness and disunity and make himself master of all Greece. He also wanted to bring his own people into the Greek cultural mainstream and thereby erase the stigma of backwardness and barbarity that other Greek speakers had placed on Macedonians.

Philip began this culturization process with his own son, Alexander, born in 356 B.C. According to Plutarch, the Macedonian king

Philip II sought to bring Greek culture to the Macedonian people.

considered that the task of training and educating his son was too important to be entrusted to the ordinary run of teachers. . . . So he sent for Aristotle, the most famous and learned of the philosophers of his time. . . . [Thanks to Aristotle, Alexander became devoted] to all kinds of learning and was a lover of books.[32]

Aristotle also instilled in his royal pupil the idea that Greeks were morally and cul-turally superior to other peoples. Alexander would later use this as a partial justification for his subjugation of foreign peoples.

Master of the Greeks

While Alexander was growing up, Philip began his methodical conquest of Greece. First, the king marched his army southward into Thessaly, taking complete control of the territory by 353 B.C. In the following year, Philip attacked and conquered

The Macedonian phalanx's frightening front wall of spear points, which Philip used to great effect, is recaptured in this painting by Peter Connolly.

Thrace, to the east of Macedonia. Soon, he controlled most of the Greek lands north of the pass of Thermopylae.

Partly because of their long-standing contempt for the Macedonians, most Greeks ignored these aggressions, believing that Philip posed no credible threat to them. However, one prominent individual, the influential Athenian orator Demosthenes, understood the danger. Starting in 351 B.C. he delivered a series of compelling speeches, some of which became known as the Philippics (because they dealt with Philip). Demosthenes called Philip a threatening barbarian and urged Athenians and other Greeks to rise up and stop the Macedonians before it was too late. "Observe, Athenians," Demosthenes said,

the height to which the fellow's insolence has soared. . . . He cannot rest content with what he has conquered; he is always taking in more, everywhere casting his net round us, while we sit idle and do nothing. When, Athenians, will you take the necessary action? What are you waiting for? Until you are compelled, I presume.[33]

For several years, most Athenians and other Greeks did not heed Demosthenes' warnings. But when Philip moved into southern Greece and took control of the shrines at Delphi in 346 B.C., many Greeks began to see that the feisty orator was right. A major showdown with Philip now seemed inevitable. Demosthenes himself almost single-handedly forged a coalition of cities, led by Athens and Thebes, with the goal of halting further Macedonian aggression.

On August 4, 338 B.C., an army of thirty-five thousand hoplites from Athens, Thebes, and other city-states met Philip's forces, numbering about thirty thousand, at Chaeronea, lying west of Thebes. At first, the Athenians, Demosthenes himself among the ranks, staged an enthusiastic charge. But the power of the Macedonian phalanx and Philip's superior battle tactics turned this attack into a retreat. Meanwhile, eighteen-year-old Alexander led the Macedonian cavalry against other elements of the allied forces. Philip's decisive victory that day gave him what he had long dreamed of—virtual mastery of Greece.

Pursuing a Glorious Destiny

Philip realized that keeping so many Greek cities under control would not be easy. He could make this task easier, he reasoned, by providing a common enemy for all Greeks to oppose. So in 337 B.C. he assembled representatives from most of the Greek states and proposed an invasion of Persia, purportedly to avenge the Persian assault on Greece in the previous century.

Philip was not fated to lead the Greeks into Asia, however. The following year he was assassinated by a disgruntled Macedonian. (Rumors suggested that Alexander and his mother, Olympias, were involved in the plot, though these have never been firmly substantiated.) So at age twenty, Alexander was king of Macedonia and "captain-general" of Greece. He continued preparations for the Persian

A Greek Calls on Philip to Invade Persia

In the autumn of 346 B.C., a Greek orator named Isocrates published an open letter to Philip II, calling on him to lead the Greek states in a war against their old enemy, Persia. It was fitting, the orator said, for Persia's vast wealth to be in the hands of Greeks, who were inherently superior to Persians. The following (an excerpt from George Norlin's translation) is Isocrates' conclusion.

I am now addressing myself to you although I am not unaware that when I am proposing this course many will look at it askance, but that when you are actually carrying it out all will rejoice in it. . . . I assert that it is incumbent on you to work for the good of the Greeks . . . and to extend your power over the greatest possible number of barbarians. For if you do . . . all men will be grateful to you.

expedition, and in 334 B.C. led an army of thirty-two thousand infantry and five thousand cavalry eastward across the Hellespont.

Before proceeding farther into Asia, Alexander stopped at the legendary site of Troy to pray to the Greek gods for victory in the coming campaign. Troy was a special place for him because he saw himself as a Homeric hero reborn. For Alexander, the conquest of Persia was not just a practical move, as it had been for his father. The young king believed that he was part god himself and that it was his destiny to conquer and rule men. Aristotle had taught him always to seek *arête*, the attainment of personal excellence. And Alexander had become obsessed with attaining glory. "Those who endure hardship and danger are the ones who achieve glory," he is quoted as saying, "and the most gratifying thing is to live with courage and to die leaving behind eternal renown."[34]

Destroyer and Builder

With this singular motto firmly in mind, between 334 and 331 B.C. Alexander led his army to victory after victory over the Persians. He captured Asia Minor, then marched southward into Palestine and besieged and captured the island city of Tyre on the Mediterranean coast. Then Alexander entered Egypt. After enduring Persian rule for two centuries, the Egyptians welcomed the young general as their liberator and the Greeks won the country without a fight.

In Egypt, as he did elsewhere, Alexander showed that he was not merely a conqueror and destroyer. He diligently sought to spread Greek language, ideas, and customs throughout the lands he defeated. He believed that this process, called Hellenization, would help to unify the many foreign peoples in his new and growing empire. So everywhere he went he ordered the construction of temples, theaters, gymnasiums, and even whole cities. In 331 B.C., near the mouth of the Nile River, he established Alexandria, which rapidly grew into one of the greatest commercial and cultural centers in the known world.

The Fall of Persia

Alexander never saw the new city rise, however. Only months after approving its ground plan, he departed Egypt and headed northeastward to resume the conquest of Persia. His expanded army now numbered forty thousand infantry and seven thousand cavalry.

Hearing that the Greeks were approaching Babylon, one of Persia's three capi-

Alexander (wearing the feathered helmet) leads his cavalry toward the waiting Persians at the Battle of the Granicus River in May 334 B.C.

Alexander's Letter to Darius

After Alexander defeated King Darius III at Issus (in southeastern Asia Minor), the two kings exchanged letters, which the later Greek historian Arrian paraphrased in his chronicle of Alexander's exploits. According to Arrian, Alexander told Darius:

Your ancestors invaded Macedonia and Greece and caused havoc in our country, though we had done nothing to provoke them. As supreme commander of all Greece, I invaded Asia because I wished to punish Persia for this act, an act which must be laid wholly to your charge. . . . By God's help I am master of your country. . . . Come to me, therefore, as you would come to the lord of the continent of Asia. . . . And in the future let any communication you wish to make with me be addressed to the King of all Asia. Do not write to me as an equal. Everything you possess is now mine; so if you should want anything, let me know in the proper terms . . . or I shall take steps to deal with you as a criminal. If, on the other hand, you wish to dispute your throne, stand and for it and do not run away. Wherever you may hide yourself, be sure I shall seek you out.

tals, the Persian king, Darius III, assembled an enormous army, perhaps three or four times larger than Alexander's. At Gaugamela, near the Tigris River in what is now central Iraq, the two forces met in a titanic, hard-fought battle. In the end, the tremendous power of the Macedonian phalanx and Alexander's keen instincts and talents as a general won the day. Darius fled the field and his remaining troops followed suit. Alexander's forces gave chase for many hours, slaughtering all those they caught. At least forty thousand Persians perished, while the Greeks lost fewer than a thousand men.

After the battle, Alexander marched to Babylon, which, after learning the outcome of Gaugamela, opened its gates without a fight. The Greeks then moved on to the other Persian capitals, Susa and Persepolis, where they also met no resistance. Alexander burned Persepolis in 330 B.C. and then continued his pursuit of Darius.

When the Macedonian king finally caught up with his adversary, he was dismayed to find that Darius had been murdered by his own followers. Apparently they had hoped that this act would win them Alexander's favor. But Alexander believed that a king should die only in battle or at the hands of another king. He had the ringleader of the traitors executed in a way meant to serve as an example. Plutarch recalled that Alexander had the tops of two straight trees bent down so that they met, and part of [the man's] body was tied to each; then, when each tree was let go, and sprang back to its upright position, the part of the body attached to it was torn off by the recoil.[35]

To India and Back

Now master of Persia, Alexander decided to continue his eastward trek and further expand his new empire. In the next four years, he marched his army thousands of miles through what are now Iran, Afghanistan, and Pakistan. All along the way, he established new cities and military forts.

In 326 B.C. the Greeks reached the borders of India. There, Alexander defeated a large Indian army equipped with some two hundred battle elephants, at the time a strange novelty in Western warfare. He may have gone on to conquer all of India, but his exhausted troops, many of whom had not seen their homes and families in many years, demanded that he turn back. Reluctantly, he led them back to Babylon, a difficult trek in which many Greeks died.

Alexander planned to continue Hellenizing the peoples he had conquered. He also began formulating his plans for further conquests, talking openly about expeditions into Arabia and Europe. But he never had a chance to implement any of these plans. At the height of his power,

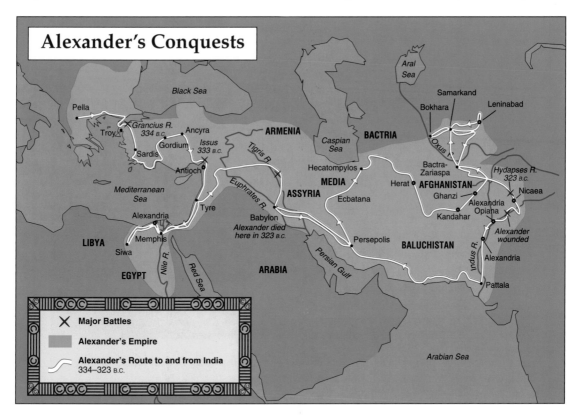

Alexander's Conquests

How Did Alexander Die?

A number of theories regarding Alexander's death have been advanced, both in ancient and modern times. One of the more popular was that he contracted malaria during his travels in southern Asia. Convincing evidence for another explanation—alcohol poisoning—has recently been presented by University of Louisville scholar Robert B. Kebric (quoted here from an unpublished paper).

There does not appear to have been any obvious reason for the onset of Alexander's fatal illness other than his heavy consumption of alcohol, which continued throughout his final days. That the most *immediate* cause of Alexander's death . . . appears to have been alcohol poisoning can hardly be a surprising revelation, since it was a common occurrence in antiquity and not infrequent within Alexander's own experience. Strong evidence concerning the death of Alexander's closest friend, Hephaestion, indicates that it was the result of heavy drinking. Elsewhere, it is written that after the death of another valued friend . . . Alexander proposed a drinking contest in which 42 of the competitors, including the victor, died from consuming too much [wine]. . . . When the medical details included as part of Arrian's and Plutarch's accounts of Alexander's death are compared with specific unrelated cases in the corpus of [the famous Greek physician] Hippocrates, the most convincing immediate reason that emerges for Alexander's death is that he *did* ultimately die from the effects of alcohol poisoning.

Macedonian officers and soldiers file past the dying Alexander in 323 B.C. Convincing evidence suggests that alcohol poisoning killed him.

Alexander suddenly fell ill, possibly of alcohol poisoning, and died at the age of thirty-three.

Alexander's Legacy

In just ten years, Alexander had created the largest empire the world had seen up to that time. It stretched from Macedonia and Greece in the west to Egypt in the south and India in the east, and encompassed more than a million square miles. But this vast political unit was not destined to last very long. In short order, Alexander's leading generals would divide it among themselves.

More enduring were the seeds of Greek culture Alexander had planted. Greek language, arts, architecture, and science continued to flourish in Alexandria and other cities that he or his agents had founded or captured. The question is whether Greek influences would have swept through the Near East either with or without Alexander. Distinguished historian Chester G. Starr points out:

Greek civilization was already expanding vigorously . . . and many men had gone to the Persian Empire as mercenaries, doctors, and traders before Alexander became king. . . . Did Alexander ride the crest of a wave which would have swept eastward anyway? Or did he himself have an important role in directing and shaping the course of events? . . . Each student of history must furnish his own answers [to these questions].[36]

One legacy of Alexander's that no one questions is the subsequent elevation of his character, talents, and deeds to legendary status. Deservedly or undeservedly, throughout the ages his name has often inspired feelings of almost superstitious awe. Typical was this statement by his principal ancient biographer, the second-century-A.D. Greek Arrian:

Never in all the world was there another like him, and therefore I cannot but feel that some power more than human was concerned in his birth . . . and there is the further evidence of the extraordinary way in which he is held, as no mere man could be, in honor and remembrance.[37]

Chapter Seven

The Hellenistic Age and "Inhabited World"

I n the three centuries following Alexander's death, Greek civilization experienced its last important phase of independent political and military power. The unique character of the age was determined in large degree by the violent events that created it. Almost immediately after Alexander's passing, a bloody power struggle erupted among his leading generals and governors. Called the Diadochoi, or Successors, they included, among others, Antipater, Craterus, Antigonus, Perdiccas, Seleucus, Eumenes, and Ptolemy (TAW-luh-mee). For nearly forty years they fought a series of costly wars that killed hundreds of thousands of people.

The wars of the Successors also completely transformed the political map of an enormous portion of the known world. The huge empire Alexander had acquired split up into a number of independent kingdoms, each ruled by one of the Successors. (A few older autonomous city-states still retained some influence, notably Athens, Rhodes, and Byzantium.) These kingdoms, which encompassed most of the Near East, carried on vigorous trade and commercial activities, so they initially enjoyed considerable economic prosperity. Their Greek ruling classes also promoted Greek language, customs, arts, and ideas.

These developments created a group of societies whose traditional Eastern languages, customs, and ideas became overlaid by a veneer of Greek ones. For this reason, modern scholars call these realms Hellenistic, meaning "Greek-like." Similarly, the historical period beginning with Alexander's death in 323 B.C. and ending with the demise of the last autonomous Greek ruler (Cleopatra VII) in 30 B.C. is called the Hellenistic Age.

The Principal Hellenistic Realms

The Hellenistic world was long dominated by three large kingdoms, which had emerged from the turmoil of the Diadochoi wars by about 280 b.c. One of these realms was the Ptolemaic kingdom. It was ruled by Ptolemy, a Macedonian nobleman, and his successors and consisted of Egypt and nearby southern Palestine. The Ptolemies did not attempt to impose a democracy or other Greek-style government in Egypt. Instead, they took the Egyptian title for king—pharaoh—and maintained the absolute monarchy that had existed in the country for dozens of centuries. The chief Ptolemaic city—Alexandria—was the greatest commercial center of the age, which enabled the Greco-Egyptian nobility and upper classes to enjoy great wealth and luxury.

The second great Hellenistic realm was the Seleucid kingdom. Ruled by Seleucus and his descendants, it consisted of much of the old Persian Empire plus parts of Asia Minor. Seleucus and his son, Antiochus I, set up many independent cities using the Greek polis as a model. These cities were allowed to decide their own local affairs. But they also had to pay heavy taxes to and obey the orders and whims of the Seleucids, who were absolute monarchs like the Ptolemies. The Seleucid city of Antioch, located on the eastern Mediterranean coast, grew large and prosperous and became the commercial rival of Alexandria.

The Macedonian kingdom was the third Hellenistic political unit. Consisting of Macedonia and parts of mainland and coastal Greece, it was ruled by the heirs of

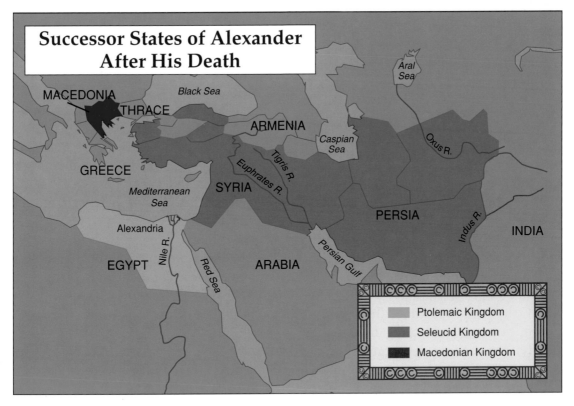

Successor States of Alexander After His Death

Ptolemaic Kingdom
Seleucid Kingdom
Macedonian Kingdom

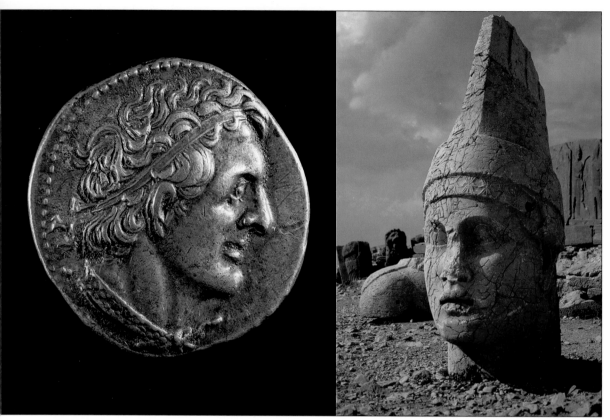

These images of two leaders of the Successor States include a coin portrait of Egypt's Ptolemy I and a stone head of Seleucia's Antiochus I.

Antigonus. The Antigonids, like the Seleucids, allowed individual poleis a certain measure of self-rule but also exerted ultimate kingly authority.

The Antigonids encountered many difficulties. First, they found it hard to govern the Greeks, who were still fiercely independent and always rebelling. Also, in 280 B.C. the Gauls, a tribal people from central Europe, invaded Greece. The warlike Gauls swept through the country, killing, burning, and looting. In 276, after nearly four years of desperate fighting, Antigonus's grandson, Antigonus II Gonatas, managed to drive the invaders

out and restore order. But peace did not last long. In the following decades, Macedonia, like the other two big Greek kingdoms, had to deal with internal rebellions by subjects unhappy with their dictatorial rulers.

The major Hellenistic kingdoms also fought one another on a regular basis. The causes of these conflicts were many and complex. Border disputes and attempts to acquire more territory were common, especially between the Ptolemies and Seleucids over possession of Syria and Palestine. Indeed, there were at least six so-called Syrian wars.

Another issue that frequently led to conflict was the need to control the communication and travel lines connecting mainland Greece and the Aegean region to various parts of the Near East. It was essential for the Seleucids and Ptolemies to maintain a steady flow of administrators, colonists, and artisans from Greece. Mercenary soldiers were even more crucial, since all of the Hellenistic rulers used them to supplement their standing armies drawn from the local citizenry. The Hellenistic monarchs also fought over access to the great trade routes that ran west to east through the Near East.

A Vast Greek Cultural Sphere

Amid all the fighting, however, the Hellenistic world became known for its commercial and cultural endeavors. Because the major states were ruled and dominated by Greeks, they shared many cultural similarities. This rapidly led to the emergence of a vast homogeneous cultural sphere stretching across the eastern Mediterranean and Near East. People came to call it the *oikoumene* (ee-koo-MEH-nee), or "inhabited world." One of its more remarkable features was that a person could travel from one end of it to the other and feel more or less at home almost anywhere within it.

Expanded Legal Rights for Women

In many parts of the Hellenistic world, women enjoyed more respect and rights than in previous eras. One piece of evidence for this is a surviving marriage contract from Greek-ruled Egypt dating from 311 B.C.—that of newlyweds Heraclides and Demetria. The document (translated by Sarah B. Pomeroy in her book on Greek women) reveals some of Demetria's apparently considerable legal rights, and also that her husband was obligated to respect them.

Heraclides takes as his lawful wife Demetria of Cos. . . . He is free; she is free. She brings with her to the marriage clothing and ornaments valued at 1000 drachmas [a considerable sum]. Heraclides shall supply to Demetria all that is suitable for a freeborn wife. . . . It shall not be lawful for Heraclides to bring home another woman for himself . . . nor to have children by another woman, nor to indulge in fraudulent [actions] against Demetria on any pretext. If Heraclides is caught doing any of these things, and Demetria proves it before three men whom they both approve, Heraclides shall return to Demetria the dowry of 1000 drachmas which she has brought, and also forfeit 1000 drachmas [of his own money]. . . . Demetria shall have the right to exact payment from Heraclides and from his property on both land and sea, as if by a legal judgment. . . . Heraclides and Demetria shall each have the right to keep a copy of the contract in their own custody, and to produce it against one another.

That does not mean that everyone who lived in the inhabited world enjoyed the same opportunities, privileges, and lifestyles, however. In fact, Hellenistic society was highly class oriented and stratified. Not surprisingly, Greeks occupied the uppermost social stratum. Greek Koine (a form of Greek that developed from the Athenian dialect) became the universal language of administration and business, and those who could not speak, read, and write it were at a severe disadvantage. "What the Successors set up were enclaves of Greco-Macedonian culture in an alien world," Peter Green points out, "governmental ghettos for a ruling elite." Despite all the temples, theaters, and gymnasiums the Greeks erected in the region, he adds,

we should never forget that it was for the Hellenized Macedonian ruling minority and its Greek supporters . . . that such home-from-home luxuries . . . [were] provided. . . . The gymnasium resembled an exclusive club; entry was highly selective . . . designed to keep out undesirables (i.e., non-Greeks).[38]

Alexandria Ascendant

The rise of these ethnic and economic elites in the leading Hellenistic states was part of a major economic transformation of the eastern Mediterranean world. Before Alexander's death, Athens had been the commercial center of that sphere for more than a century. But as the Ptolemaic and Seleucid kingdoms gained prominence, the center of trade shifted to Alexandria and Antioch. And although Athens remained an important center of culture and learning, it and many of the other mainland Greek poleis underwent an economic decline.

In contrast, Alexandria was a new and prosperous center of trade, commerce, and learning. Its population steadily increased during the Hellenistic period, eventually reaching seven hundred thousand or more. This was partly because people from many other cities and countries found its modern, cosmopolitan atmosphere attractive. The third-century-B.C. Greek poet Herodas said of Alexandria:

Every object that grows or is made abounds [there]: wealth, wrestling schools . . . tranquility, renown . . . philosophers, gold, pretty young boys, the Museum, fine wine, every luxury you could want, and women in more numbers than the heavens boast stars, for comeliness [beauty] the equal of the goddesses.[39]

The "Museum" mentioned by Herodas was not a building housing old or rare artifacts. Rather, it was a university-like center of scientific research. Ptolemy I began building it in about 300 B.C., and he and his son subsequently invited the greatest scholars in the known world to live, study, experiment, and lecture there. In addition to living quarters for these scholars, the facility featured lecture halls, a library, a botanical garden, a small zoo, and a theater. Adjoining the Museum was Alexandria's Great Library, which early in Hellenistic times was already the largest library in the known world. It contained

Ptolemy II Philadelphus visits the great library at Alexandria, an institution his father began and that he completed.

as many as seven hundred thousand manuscripts.

Hellenistic Science

Libraries and centers of learning appeared in other Hellenistic cities as well. These facilities nurtured numerous brilliant thinkers who created a sort of scientific renaissance that would not be matched until modern times. As noted classical scholar Michael Grant puts it:

> Mathematics, astronomy, geography, and medicine flourished in the Hellenistic Age as never before. For one thing, while . . . the old city-state governments had never spent much money on research, the new monarchs [of the Hellenistic kingdoms] felt differently. So the richer among these kings proceeded to establish more permanent foundations for learning . . . [such as] the Museum.[40]

The work of the Hellenistic Greek scientists was often truly impressive. In the early third century B.C., for instance, the astronomer Aristarchus of Samos suggested that the other planets are spheres like Earth and the moon. Furthermore, he said, Earth does not rest at the center of the universe, as most people in his day believed.

One of the many brilliant Greek scientists who lived and worked at Alexandria was Hipparchus, here depicted looking through a lensless tube.

He proposed instead that the sun is at the center and that Earth and the planets revolve around it.

Though shown in early modern times to be correct, this theory was too revolutionary for its time. And most other Greek scientists rejected it. Thus, in the following century, another noted Greek astronomer, Hipparchus of Nicaea, promoted the traditional Earth-centered theory. However, Hipparchus did make some correct and important astronomical discoveries and calculations. He measured the distance from Earth to the moon with an error of only 5 percent, for example. He also invented the now familiar system of lines of longitude and latitude for use on maps of both the sky and Earth.

The greatest of the Hellenistic scientists was Archimedes, who was born in Syracuse in the early third century B.C. His *On the Sphere and Cylinder, Measurement of a Circle, On the Equilibrium of Planes, The Sand-Reckoner, On Floating Bodies*, and other works were clear, logical, and largely correct demonstrations of some of the most important mathematical and mechanical concepts, including the fundamental laws of levers and floating bodies.

One of Archimedes' most famous discoveries came one day when he was sitting in a bathtub. As he and countless others had noticed before, when he submerged himself the water level rose and his body appeared to weigh less. Suddenly, he deduced why this occurs. A floating body, he realized, loses weight in direct proportion to the weight of the water it displaces. This later became known as the principle of buoyancy.

Archimedes also experimented with new ways to make physical labor easier. In one of his most celebrated demonstrations, he had a large dry-docked ship loaded with supplies and people. To the ship he attached ropes that ran to a complicated mechanism made up of pulleys and levers. Then, as Plutarch told it, he

seated himself at some distance away and without using any noticeable force, but merely exerting traction with his hand through [the] system of pulleys, he drew the vessel towards him with as smooth and even a motion as if she were gliding through the water.[41]

A New Appreciation for the Individual

Part of the driving force of Hellenistic science was the search for the underlying truths of the natural world and how people fit in to the scheme of things. This spirit was mirrored by a meaningful shift in social attitudes about people, especially the individual human being. There was an increased appreciation and respect for the individual, including his or her intellect, emotions, talents, needs, and happiness.

This new emphasis on the individual found concrete expression in the arts, as the poets, sculptors, and painters of the age achieved levels of vividness and realism unknown before. In prior eras, artists had almost always chosen divine or heroic subjects, which were portrayed in ideal situations and poses. In Hellenistic times, by contrast, archaeologist William R. Biers writes, "for the first time all classes of society and all gradations of physical condition were realistically shown, and often caricatured."[42]

Another striking development was that the new preoccupation with the individual applied to women as well as men. The social position and literary and artistic portrayal of women "underwent an unprecedented transformation that was one of the most remarkable evolutionary changes of the age,"[43] Grant remarks. Although most women were still excluded from political life, large numbers of them enjoyed expanded economic rights and clout. Documents written on papyrus, mostly discovered in Egypt, show that women in that region (both Greek and native Egyptian) regularly gave and received loans; bought and sold land, slaves, and other property; inherited and bequeathed property and other legacies; and even made their own marriage contracts, perhaps sometimes without the consent of their fathers or other guardians. (Not all Hellenistic women experienced the same degree of liberation. Improvements in Athenian women's lives appear to have been minimal as compared to those of their Ptolemaic and Macedonian counterparts, for example. And poorer women continued to have fewer opportunities than well-to-do ones.)

Climax of a Doomed World

In many ways the early Hellenistic era witnessed the climax of ancient Greek civilization. Greeks controlled huge sections of the known world, enjoyed unprecedented prosperity, and made significant social, artistic, literary, and scientific strides. Also, the military system employed by the Hellenistic states, spearheaded by the dreaded Macedonian phalanx, was widely viewed as invincible. Had the Greeks not continued to fight among themselves, as they had for centuries, perhaps a powerful "United States of Greece" may have eventually emerged. Such a political-military entity would have had the potential to

This modern drawing depicts the famous event in which the inventor Archimedes moved a ship using only human muscle power.

An Inventor
Who Hated Inventing

As history has shown, Archimedes proved to be a brilliant inventor. However, inventing was always secondary to him, as he much preferred mathematics and other aspects of theoretical science over practical applications of his theories. Plutarch explained this in his Life of Marcellus, *translated in* Makers of Rome.

He was a man who possessed such exalted ideals . . . and such a wealth of scientific knowledge that, although his inventions had earned [him] a reputation for almost superhuman intellectual power, he would not deign to leave behind him any writings on his mechanical discoveries. He regarded the business of engineering . . . as ignoble and sordid activity, and he concentrated his ambition exclusively upon those speculations whose beauty and subtlety were untainted by the claims of necessity. These studies, he believed, are incomparably superior to any others, since here the grandeur and beauty of the subject matter vie for our admiration with the cogency and precision of the methods of proof.

dominate all of Europe and beyond for a very long time.

However, the reality was that the Greeks did remain disunited and continued to exhaust themselves in debilitating wars. As had happened before, in the late Classical Age, this left them vulnerable to attack from an opportunistic outside force. This time the threat came from a long way off and was totally unexpected. In the opening section of his famous history book, the second-century-B.C. Greek Polybius named that threat and described the speed at which it crept across the horizon of the doomed Greek world:

There can surely be nobody so . . . apathetic in his outlook that he has no desire to discover by what means . . . the Romans succeeded in less than fifty-three years in bringing under their rule almost the whole of the inhabited world, an achievement that is without parallel in human history.[44]

The Greeks' Decline and Their Legacy

The Roman conquest of the Greek lands was frighteningly swift. This was due in part to the fact that Rome, which had taken control of almost all of the western Mediterranean world by 201 B.C., had developed a highly effective military machine. The key to its success was its flexibility. On the battlefield the Roman army broke down in many small, mobile units that were able to outmaneuver and thereby nullify the power of the more monolithic and inflexible Greek phalanx.

The superiority of the Roman military became evident soon after Rome invaded Macedonia in 200 B.C. Three years later, at Cynoscephalae (in northeastern Greece) a Roman army decimated Macedonia's supposedly invincible phalanx. After that, the Hellenistic states, which continued to squabble among themselves even as they were being overrun, fell one by one. Rome controlled most of the eastern Mediterranean by 146 B.C. In that year a Roman general brutally destroyed the once great city of Corinth as an object lesson to other Greeks who might dare to rebel.

Farther south, the Ptolemaic kingdom remained more or less intact for another century. But by this time it had been reduced to a third-rate power cowering in Rome's enormous shadow, and its days as an independent political entity were clearly numbered. Finally, in 31 B.C., the Romans defeated Cleopatra, last of the Ptolemies, and her Roman ally and lover Mark Antony in a great sea battle near Actium (in western Greece). The following year the lovers committed suicide, and Rome annexed Egypt, making it the newest province of its growing empire. It was the Romans, and not the Greeks, therefore, who subsequently went on to unite the whole Mediterranean world into a vast commonwealth administered by one central government.

The Greek Spirit

Fortunately for later generations, however, many aspects of Greek culture survived the fall of the Greek nation-states. And ironically, the main instrument of that survival was the same force that had deprived the Greeks of their independence—Rome. Indeed, in the fullness of time, the Hellenization of Rome proved more profound and ultimately more influential than the Romanization of Greece. The highly practical Romans, who so often adopted the most attractive and useful aspects of the peoples they conquered, were greatly affected by Greek customs, arts, and ideas. In literature, architecture, painting, law, religion, philosophy, and numerous other areas, the Romans incorporated Greek styles and concepts. The result was the Greco-Roman cultural fusion that eventually came to be called "classical" civilization.

Many centuries after the Roman Empire disintegrated in the fifth and sixth centuries, Europeans rediscovered classical civilization and its ancient Greek underpinnings. In this way, Greek culture and ideas came to strongly shape the modern Western world. Today, examples abound at every turn. Thousands of modern banks, government buildings, and other structures employ the familiar columns and triangular gables of classical Greek temple

An Unheeded Call for Greek Unity

Rome's conquest of Greece was possible in large part because the Greeks never presented a united front against the Roman onslaught. At least a few Greeks recognized how essential unity was, as evidenced by the surviving words of a Greek orator named Agelaus of Aetolia. In 213 B.C. he delivered this warning (preserved by Polybius in his Histories*), which most of his fellow Greeks ignored.*

It would be best of all if the Greeks never went to war with one another, if they could regard it as the greatest gift of the gods for them to speak with one voice, and could join hands like men who are crossing a river; in this way they could unite to repulse the incursions of the barbarians and to preserve themselves and their cities. But if we have no hope of achieving such a degree of unity for the whole of the country, let me impress on you [the disturbing reality] . . . of the huge armies which have been mobilized, and vast scale of the war [the Second Punic War, fought between Rome and Carthage] which is now being waged in the west. . . . Whether the Carthaginians defeat the Romans or the Romans the Carthaginians, the victors will by no means be satisfied with the sovereignty of Italy and Sicily, but will come here [to the Greek lands], and will advance both their forces and their ambitions beyond the bounds of justice.

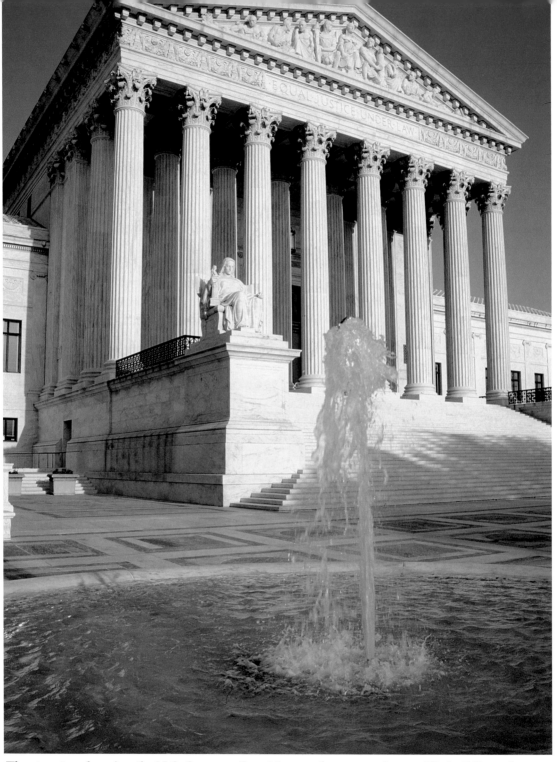

The structure housing the U.S. Supreme Court is one of many modern public buildings that utilize ancient Greek temple architecture.

During the colorful opening ceremonies of the 2004 summer Olympic Games, held in Athens, an actor portrays Alexander the Great.

architecture. And every four years, the world's nations compete in the Olympic Games, inspired by the original Greek version. Likewise, modern theater and drama would not exist without the Greeks. Nor would democratic governments and voting for one's leaders exist; nor gymnasiums and track and field competitions; literary genres like the novel, essay, biography, and history book; philosophical enquiry; and scientific exploration of atoms, plants and animals, and the vast universe lying beyond Earth.

In these and other ways, part of the spirit of the ancient Greeks, a people long dead, remains, and perhaps will always remain interwoven in the lives and thoughts of the living in each new generation. It is the spirit not only of human worth and love of freedom and independence but also of the relentless quest for beauty and truth. The Greeks sought to discover and understand the underlying truths of nature and of themselves as well. As long as people reach out to know, to learn, to understand, and to find the truth, the Greek spirit will never die.

Notes

Introduction: The Intrinsic Worth of the Individual

1. C.M. Bowra, *Classical Greece.* New York: Time-Life, 1965, p. 11.
2. C.E. Robinson, *Hellas: A Short History of Ancient Greece.* Boston: Beacon, 1957, pp. 195–96, 198.

Chapter 1: The Birth of Greek Civilization

3. Maitland A. Edey, *Lost World of the Aegean.* New York: Time-Life, 1975, p. 78.
4. Plutarch, *Life of Theseus*, in *The Rise and Fall of Athens: Nine Greek Lives by Plutarch*, trans. Ian Scott-Kilvert. New York: Penguin, 1960, pp. 25–26.
5. Edey, *Lost World of the Aegean*, p. 109.
6. Thomas R. Martin, *Ancient Greece: From Prehistoric to Hellenistic Times.* New Haven, CT: Yale University Press, 1996, pp. 31–32.

Chapter 2: The Rise of City-States

7. Sarah B. Pomeroy et al. *Ancient Greece: A Political, Social, and Cultural History.* New York: Oxford University Press, 1999, pp. 47– 48.
8. Bowra, *Classical Greece*, p. 17.

Chapter 3: Democracy and Empire: Athens Ascendant

9. Quoted in Thucydides, *The Peloponnesian War*, trans. Rex Warner. New York: Penguin, 1972, p. 148.
10. Malcolm F. McGregor, *The Athenians and Their Empire.* Vancouver: University of British Columbia Press, 1987, p. 116.
11. Herodotus, *The Histories*, trans. Aubrey de Sélincourt. New York: Penguin, 1972, p. 382.
12. Herodotus, *Histories*, p. 429.
13. Herodotus, *Histories*, p. 504.
14. Aeschylus, *The Persians*, in *Aeschylus: Prometheus Bound, The Suppliants, Seven Against Thebes, The Persians*, trans. Philip Vellacott. Baltimore, MD: Penguin, 1961, p. 133.
15. Thucydides, *Peloponnesian War*, pp. 45–46.
16. Thucydides, *Peloponnesian War*, p. 93.
17. Thucydides, *Peloponnesian War*, p. 35.

Chapter 4: Society and Culture in Classical Athens

18. Euripides, *Hecuba 331–332,* passage translated by Don Nardo.
19. Sue Blundell, *Women in Ancient Greece.* Cambridge, MA: Harvard University Press, 1995, pp. 122–23.
20. Robert Flaceliere, *Daily Life in Greece at the Time of Pericles*, trans. Peter Green. London: Phoenix, 1996, p. 97.
21. Quoted in Lycurgus, *Against Leocrates*, in J.O. Butt, trans., *Minor Attic Orators.* Cambridge, MA: Harvard

University Press, 1962, p. 21.

22. Plutarch, *Life of Pericles*, in *Rise and Fall of Athens*, pp. 178–79.
23. Quoted in Peter Green, *The Parthenon*. New York: Newsweek, 1973, p. 155.
24. Quoted in Thucydides, *Peloponnesian War*, pp. 147–48.

Chapter 5: Incessant Warfare Exhausts the Greeks

25. Thucydides, *Peloponnesian War*, p. 37.
26. Quoted in Thucydides, *Peloponnesian War*, pp. 73–74.
27. Thucydides, *Peloponnesian War*, pp. 152–53.
28. Thucydides, *Peloponnesian War*, p. 537.
29. Peter Connolly, *Greece and Rome at War*. London: Greenhill, 1998, p. 51.
30. Xenophon, *Hellenica*, published as *A History of My Times*, trans. Rex Warner. New York: Penguin, 1979, p. 403.

Chapter 6: The Conquests of Philip and Alexander

31. Peter Green, *Alexander of Macedon, 356–323 B.C.: A Historical Biography*. Berkeley: University of California Press, 1991, p. 6.
32. Plutarch, *Life of Alexander*, in *The Age of Alexander: Nine Greek Lives by Plutarch*, trans. Ian Scott-Kilvert. New York: Penguin, 1973, pp. 359–60.
33. Demosthenes, *First Philippic*, in Demosthenes, *Olynthiacs, Philippics, Minor Speeches*, trans. J.H. Vince. Cambridge, MA: Harvard University Press, 1962, pp. 73–75.

34. Quoted in Arrian, *Anabasis Alexandri* 5.26, passage translated by Don Nardo.
35. Plutarch, *Alexander*, in *Age of Alexander*, p. 301.
36. Chester G. Starr, *The Ancient Greeks*. New York: Oxford University Press, 1971, p. 165.
37. Arrian, *Anabasis Alexandri*, published as *The Campaigns of Alexander*, trans. Aubrey de Sélincourt. New York: Penguin, 1971, p. 398.

Chapter 7: The Hellenistic Age and "Inhabited World"

38. Peter Green, *Alexander to Actium: The Historical Evolution of the Hellenistic Age*. Berkeley: University of California Press, 1990, p. 319.
39. Herodas, *Mimiambi*, trans. Peter Green in *Alexander to Actium*, p. 245.
40. Michael Grant, *From Alexander to Cleopatra: The Hellenistic World*. New York: Charles Scribner's Sons, 1982, p. 151.
41. Plutarch, *Life of Marcellus*, in *Makers of Rome: Nine Lives by Plutarch*, trans. Ian Scott-Kilvert. New York: Penguin, 1965, p. 99.
42. William R. Biers, *The Archaeology of Greece*. Ithaca, NY: Cornell University Press, 1996, p. 286.
43. Grant, *From Alexander to Cleopatra*, p. xiii.
44. Polybius, *Histories*, published as *Polybius: The Rise of the Roman Empire*, trans. Ian Scott-Kilvert. New York: Penguin, 1979, p. 41.

For Further Reading

Books

Peter Connolly, *The Greek Armies.* Morristown, NJ: Silver Burdette, 1979. A fine, detailed study of Greek armor, weapons, and battle tactics, filled with colorful, accurate illustrations. Highly recommended.

Robert B. Kebric, *Greek People.* Mountain View, CA: Mayfield, 2001. A superb overview of major ancient Greek figures from all walks of life.

Michael Kerrigan, *Ancient Greece and the Mediterranean.* New York: Dorling Kindersley, 2001. This brief but useful overview of ancient Greek civilization, aimed at beginners in the subject, is filled with stunning color photos of locales and artifacts.

Don Nardo, *Greek Temples.* New York: Franklin Watts, 2002. A colorfully illustrated overview of how Greek temples were built and used. Written for younger readers.

———, *Greenhaven Encyclopedia of Greek and Roman Mythology.* San Diego: Greenhaven, 2002. Contains hundreds of short but informative articles on Greek myths, gods, heroes, and the myth tellers and their works.

———, *Women of Ancient Greece.* San Diego: Lucent, 2000. A detailed look at all aspects of the lives of women in the ancient Greek city-states.

Web Sites

Hellenic Museum and Cultural Center, "A Day in the Life of an Ancient Greek" (www.hellenicmuseum.org/exhibits/dayinlife.html). A useful, easy-to-read general source for ancient Greek life, including clothes, food, sports, art, and more.

PBS, "The Greeks: Crucible of Civilization" (www.pbs.org/empires/the greeks). Excellent online resource based on the acclaimed PBS show. Has numerous links to sites containing information about ancient Greek history and culture.

Tufts University Department of the Classics, "Perseus Project" (www.perseus.tufts.edu). The most comprehensive online source about ancient Greece, with hundreds of links to all aspects of Greek history, life, and culture, supported by numerous photos of artifacts.

Works Consulted

Major Works

Paul Cartledge, *The Spartans: The World of the Warrior-Heroes of Ancient Greece, from Utopia to Crisis and Collapse.* New York: Overlook, 2003. A masterful overview of Sparta and its relations with other Greek states by the leading scholar of ancient Sparta.

Rodney Castleden, *Minoans: Life in Bronze Age Crete.* New York: Routledge, 1993. A good general synopsis of the Minoans.

J.R. Ellis, *Philip II and Macedonian Imperialism.* New York: Thames and Hudson, 1977. One of the best modern studies of the rise of Philip II and Macedonia.

Charles Freeman, *The Greek Achievement: The Foundation of the Western World.* New York: Viking, 1999. A well-written overview of ancient Greek civilization, touching on cultural endeavors as well as history.

Michael Grant, *The Rise of the Greeks.* New York: Macmillan, 1987. A superb examination of the rise of city-states in Greece, with detailed studies of nearly fifty separate states.

Peter Green, *Alexander of Macedon, 356–323 B.C.: A Historical Biography.* Berkeley: University of California Press, 1991. One of the two or three best available overviews of Alexander and his exploits by one of the leading classical historians of the past century.

———, *Alexander to Actium: The Historical Evolution of the Hellenistic Age.* Berkeley: University of California Press, 1990. This huge tome is the most comprehensive study of Greece's Hellenistic Age written to date.

———, *The Greco-Persian Wars.* Berkeley: University of California Press, 1996. An excellent overview of the Greek repulse of Persia from 490 to 479 B.C.

Victor D. Hanson, *The Wars of the Ancient Greeks and Their Invention of Western Military Culture.* London: Cassell, 1999. A fine general study of ancient Greek military methods, battles, and wars.

Donald Kagan, *The Peloponnesian War.* New York: Viking, 2003. A renowned scholar masterfully summarizes the long and devastating conflict that involved nearly all of the city-states.

Thomas R. Martin, *Ancient Greece: From Prehistoric to Hellenistic Times.* New Haven, CT: Yale University Press, 1996. One of the best general overviews of Greek history and culture on the market.

Sarah B. Pomeroy et al., *Ancient Greece: A Political, Social, and Cultural History.* New York: Oxford University Press, 1999. A very well-organized, detailed, and insightful summary of ancient Greek civilization.

Graham Shipley, *The Greek World After Alexander, 323–30 B.C.* London: Routledge, 2000. A superior overview of the Hellenistic Age, Successor states, and decline of Greece.

Carol G. Thomas and Craig Conant, *Citadel to City-State: The Transformation of Greece, 1200–700 B.C.E.* Indianapolis: Indiana University Press, 1999. This examination of Greece in the Dark and Archaic ages is well written and worthwhile.

Other Important Works

Primary Sources

Aeschylus, *The Persians*, in *Aeschylus: Prometheus Bound, The Suppliants, Seven Against Thebes, The Persians.* Trans. Philip Vellacott. Baltimore, MD: Penguin, 1961.

Arrian, *Anabasis Alexandri*, published as *The Campaigns of Alexander.* Trans. Aubrey de Sélincourt. New York: Penguin, 1971.

J.O. Butt, trans., *Minor Attic Orators.* Cambridge, MA: Harvard University Press, 1962.

Demosthenes, *Olynthiacs, Philippics, Minor Speeches.* Trans. J.H. Vince. Cambridge, MA: Harvard University Press, 1962.

Diodorus Siculus, *Library of History.* Various trans. 12 vols. Cambridge, MA: Harvard University Press, 1962–1967.

Herodotus, *The Histories.* Trans. Aubrey de Sélincourt. New York: Penguin, 1972.

Isocrates, surviving works in George Norlin and Larue Van Hook, trans., *Isocrates.* 3 vols. Cambridge, MA: Harvard University Press, 1928–1954.

Pausanias, *Guide to Greece.* Trans. Peter Levi. 2 vols. New York: Penguin, 1971.

Plutarch, *Parallel Lives*, excerpted in *The Rise and Fall of Athens: Nine Greek Lives by Plutarch.* Trans. Ian Scott-Kilvert. New York: Penguin, 1960; also excerpted in *The Age of Alexander: Nine Greek Lives by Plutarch.* Trans. Ian Scott-Kilvert. New York: Penguin, 1973; and *Makers of Rome: Nine Lives by Plutarch.* Trans. Ian Scott-Kilvert. New York: Penguin, 1965.

———, assorted works in *Plutarch on Sparta.* Trans. Richard J.A. Talbert. New York: Penguin, 1988.

Polybius, *Histories*, published as *Polybius: The Rise of the Roman Empire.* Trans. Ian Scott-Kilvert. New York: Penguin, 1979.

Thucydides, *The Peloponnesian War.* Trans. Rex Warner. New York: Penguin, 1972.

Xenophon, *Hellenica*, published as *A History of My Times.* Trans. Rex Warner. New York: Penguin, 1979.

———, assorted works in *Scripta Minora.* Trans. E.C. Marchant. Cambridge, MA: Harvard University Press, 1993.

Modern Sources

Lesley Adkins and Roy A. Adkins, *Handbook to Life in Ancient Greece.* New York: Facts On File, 1997.

William R. Biers, *The Archaeology of Greece.* Ithaca, NY: Cornell University Press, 1996.

Sue Blundell, *Women in Ancient Greece.* Cambridge, MA: Harvard University Press, 1995.

C.M. Bowra, *Classical Greece.* New York: Time-Life, 1965.

Peter Connolly, *Greece and Rome at War.* London: Greenhill, 1998.

J.K. Davies, *Democracy and Classical Greece.* Cambridge, MA: Harvard University

Press, 1993.

Robert Drews, *The End of the Bronze Age: Changes in Warfare and the Catastrophe ca. 200 B.C.* Princeton, NJ: Princeton University Press, 1993.

Maitland A. Edey, *Lost World of the Aegean.* New York: Time-Life, 1975.

J. Lesley Fitton, *Discovery of the Greek Bronze Age.* London: British Museum, 1995.

Robert Flaceliere, *Daily Life in Greece at the Time of Pericles.* Trans. Peter Green. London: Phoenix, 1996.

Michael Grant, *The Classical Greeks.* New York: Scribner's, 1989.

———, *From Alexander to Cleopatra: The Hellenistic World.* New York: Charles Scribner's Sons, 1982.

Peter Green, *The Parthenon.* New York: Newsweek, 1973.

N.G.L. Hammond, *A History of Greece to 322 B.C.* Oxford, England: Clarendon, 1986.

———, *Philip of Macedon.* Baltimore, MD: Johns Hopkins University Press, 1994.

Victor D. Hanson, *The Other Greeks: The Family Farm and the Agrarian Roots of Western Civilization.* New York: Simon and Schuster, 1995.

———, *The Western Way of War: Infantry Battle in Classical Greece.* New York: Oxford University Press, 1989.

Donald Kagan, *Pericles of Athens and the Birth of Democracy.* New York: Free Press, 1991.

Robert B. Kebric, "The Death of Alexander the Great: Alcohol Poisoning and Some Case Studies from Hippocrates," unpublished paper 2004.

J.V. Luce, *Lost Atlantis: New Light on an Old Legend.* New York: McGraw-Hill, 1969.

Malcolm F. McGregor, *The Athenians and Their Empire.* Vancouver: University of British Columbia Press, 1987.

Christian Meier, *Athens: Portrait of a City in Its Golden Age.* Trans. Robert and Rita Kimber. New York: Henry Holt, 1998.

Sarah B. Pomeroy, *Goddesses, Whores, Wives, and Slaves: Women in Classical Antiquity.* New York: Shocken, 1995.

C.E. Robinson, *Hellas: A Short History of Ancient Greece.* Boston: Beacon, 1957.

Nicholas Sekunda, *Marathon 490 B.C.: The First Persian Invasion of Greece.* Oxford, England: Osprey, 2002.

Nicholas Sekunda and John Warry, *Alexander the Great: His Armies and Campaigns, 334–323 B.C.* London: Osprey, 1998.

A.M. Snodgrass, *Archaic Greece.* Berkeley: University of California Press, 1980.

Philip de Souza, *The Greek and Persian Wars, 499–386 B.C.* London: Osprey, 2003.

Chester G. Starr, *The Ancient Greeks.* New York: Oxford University Press, 1971.

———, *A History of the Ancient World.* New York: Oxford University Press, 1991.

William Taylour, *The Mycenaeans.* London: Thames and Hudson, 1983.

George D. Wilcoxon, *Athens Ascendant.* Ames: Iowa State University Press, 1979.

Index

Thera, 21–23
Thermopylae, 44, 77, 89
Thessaly, 76
Thomas, Carol G., 22
Thucydides, 47, 49–50, 63, 66–67, 69
Tigris River, 80
Tiryns, 20, 26
tools, 15, 28
trade
    Alexandria and, 88
    economic prosperity and, 51, 84
    embargo of, 67
    networks and, 28–29, 87
    traders and, 15–17, 52–53, 83
travel lines, 87
tributes, 43
Trojan horse, 24
Trojan War, 23–24
Troy, 12, 16–17, 23–24
tyrants, 31–32
Tyre, 78

University of Louisville, 82
Vanderbilt University, 25
Vellacott, Philip, 47
Ventris, Michael, 27

wanax, 22
warlords, 23, 28
weapons, 15, 28
women, 53
    government involvement and, 14, 29, 55
    legal rights of, 87, 91
    marriage of, 53–54
    Minotaur and, 18
worshipper, 35, 61
worth, individual, 12–14, 91–92
writing, 27–28, 55, 65, 93

Xenophon, 73
Xerxes, 44, 47

Zeus, 37, 72

Picture Credits

Cover: Wolfgang Kaehler/CORBIS
akg-images, 13, 30, 66, 90, 92
akg-images/Electa, 89
akg-images/Peter Connolly, 19, 20, 24, 25, 33, 34, 40, 49 (both), 52, 57, 58 (upper left, middle), 59 (all), 60 (both), 76, 79
The Art Archive, 17, 35
Art Resource, N.Y., 75
Alinari/Art Resource, N.Y., 11 (lower right), 68
Bildarchiv Preussischer Kulturbesitz/Art Resource, N.Y., 56 (both)
Erich Lessing/Art Resource, N.Y., 10 (upper left), 36, 86 (left)
HIP/Art Resource, N.Y., 23
Scala/Art Resource, N.Y., 41, 48

Bridgeman Art Library, 58 (lower left)
© Bettmann/CORBIS, 10 (upper right), 11 (lower left & right), 26
© Mike Blake/CORBIS, 97
© Ed Bohon/CORBIS, 96
Burstein Collection/CORBIS, 10 (lower right)
© Gianni Dagli Orti/CORBIS, 10 (lower left)
© Royalty Free/CORBIS, 86 (right)
Time-Life Pictures/Getty Images, 42, 46, 69
Mary Evans Picture Library, 72
Don Nardo, 18, 21
North Wind Picture Archive, 45, 65, 82
Steve Zmina, 32, 71

About the Author

Historian Don Nardo has written or edited numerous volumes about the ancient Greek world, including *Greek and Roman Sport, The Age of Pericles, The Parthenon, Life in Ancient Athens, The Decline and Fall of Ancient Greece*, and literary companions to the works of Homer, Euripides, and Sophocles. He resides with his wife, Christine, in Massachusetts.